America in
Modern European Literature

From Image to Metaphor

The publication of this work has been aided by a
grant from the Andrew W. Mellon Foundation

America in
Modern European Literature

From Image to Metaphor

Richard Ruland

New York: NEW YORK UNIVERSITY PRESS · 1976

PN56.3
U5
R8

Library of Congress Cataloging in Publication Data
Ruland, Richard, 1932-
    America in modern European literature.

    Includes bibliographical references and index.
    1. United States in literature. 2. Literature,
Modern—History and criticism. I. Title.
PN56.3.U5R8   809.3'9'32   74-29376
ISBN 0-8147-7364-8

For Barbara

O my America! my new-found-land,
My kingdome, safeliest when with one man man'd
My Myne of precious stones, My Emperie,
How blest am I in this discovering thee!
To enter in these bonds, is to be free . . . .

—John Donne, "To His Mistris Going to Bed"

Madeleine c'est mon Nöel
C'est mon Amérique à moi . . . .

Madeleine c'est mon horizon
C'est mon Amérique à moi . . . .

  —Jacques Brel, "Madeleine"

Preface

Any large subject invites study from a variety of viewpoints. When one enters the neighborhood of such subjects, therefore, he is wise to describe his own angle of vision at the outset. The question he means to ask will necessarily determine his methodology and the scope of his investigation and it will with similar inevitability define its limitations. I inquire here into an aspect of the New World's impact on the Old. That impact has been enormous; it raises questions whose number and complexity can perhaps be matched only by asking how Europe has influenced and continues to influence America. (For an explanation of my appropriation of "America" throughout to refer almost exclusively to the United States, see p. 7.) No single student can hope to touch all the political and economic, the racial, social, and religious implications of such subjects. In the aesthetic sphere alone there have been countless different kinds of influence: of one author on another, of an entire literature on an author or generation of authors, of political or cultural movements in one country attracting or repelling the artists of another, of personal or national imperatives drawing an artist's attention to a distant land with the hope of finding there solutions to the problems—personal, political, aesthetic—that face him at home. Each of these areas might well call to mind particular disciplines and suitable methodology.

In such a context my question has been a modest one. I have looked at important works of modern European literature and asked what part America has played in their construction. I have kept my inquiry as purely aesthetic as I could and I have drawn primarily upon the methods of critical exegesis. Why has this author chosen to introduce America or Americans into this particular work? How has his choice helped him solve the aesthetic problem he faced at this point in this book? The European writer of the twentieth century inherited rich materials in the associations history had drawn around the idea of America. As an artist, he often found uses for these associations. In the chapters of Part Two, I discuss several examples of such uses, always with an eye to the ultimate aesthetic success of the whole poem, novel, or play and the contribution made by the American metaphor to that success.

There are questions closely related to the one I ask, questions I have not meant to raise except in defining the periphery of my subject. The America my authors draw upon rarely resembles an actual United States; such geographical, historical, or political validity is at any rate not central to the uses I examine here. As Edmundo O'Gorman has argued, this America of the imagination was more an invention than a discovery, an invention that long predated Columbus. Such an imagined America has had a history, a history that brought it richly laden into the twentieth century where its development continued—often in directions pointed by the books I discuss here. But my primary subject is not the origin and history of Europe's idea of America. There has been a great deal of work by many hands on this question, and still there is no thoroughly satisfactory discussion available, nor even an adequate bibliographical guide to the subject. I have discussed O'Gorman's thesis and drawn together in essay form materials and references which may help launch such an inquiry. The essay relates to my central concern in this book, and I think its inclusion may prove useful in a supplementary way. But it should be distinguished from that concern, and so I have set it apart as Part One.

It is a similar desire to keep my topic distinct that leads me to the word *metaphor*. Some would doubtless prefer *concept* or *image*, but these point more to what is thought or envisioned than to what might be done artistically with the fact of their existence; as terms they are most appropriate to the survey in Part One. *Symbol* comes closer to the mark, but here again we are usually drawn rather swiftly toward the thing symbolized. Perhaps the best alternative—if one is sought—is *myth*. When I started this book more than a dozen years ago, *myth* seemed a very tired word indeed. Perhaps it could be refurbished decently now; but even though we often direct our attention to the uses to which the myth is put rather than to its narrative content, it is this very narrative component which renders the term less than satisfactory for my present purposes. I do not wish to suggest typical American stories—the triumph of good through the courage of the white-hatted cowboy, the reward of industry and integrity through marriage with the boss's daughter. *Myth* means too much. I want simply to examine in their rhetorical contexts the function of richly evocative imaginative constructs. For this *metaphor* seems the most adequate term.

In an effort to discriminate further I have contrasted *metaphor* with *local color*, an image used for what it can be made to suggest as against materials transcribed without significant imaginative transformation. I have selected one of the great archetypal metaphors and asked why many of the most profound writers of our time have used it—what it has helped them to do and to say. Such questions concern the creative imagination; they affirm sharply that neither this book nor the writing examined in it is directly concerned with the United States. The taste for the exotic, on the other hand, often leads local colorists and their audience to savor the distant and foreign solely because it *is* different. The contrast can be seen by comparing Puccini's adaptation of Belasco's play (based on a Bret Harte story), *The Girl of the Golden West,* and Dvorak's New World Symphony. Puccini's use of the American West becomes unintentional farce because the opera gains nothing, either literally or metaphorically, from the details of its American locale. Dvorak, on the other hand, when criticized for not describing America more faithfully in his music—as he often was—always replied that his purpose had been to retain his native point of view and make a Slavic statement through the medium of American folk melodies: "In the Negro melodies of America I find all that is needed for a great and noble school of music. . . . There is nothing in the whole range of composition which cannot be supplied from this source. . . ." It is this contribution of America to creative art that occupies the following pages. Dvorak saw his artistic purposes as superior to simple representation of

American idiosyncrasies. When Joseph Glenville wrote "That there is an *America* of secrets yet to be learned . . . is more than conjecture," he meant only to indicate the boundless future he saw for scientific inquiry. And what reader of the poem which supplies my epigraph ever thought Donne was talking about America?

There has been a staggering amount of European travel and descriptive journalism produced to satisfy curiosity about America. I have not been interested in books about America but only in those which use America creatively. This study should be distinguished as well from at least three other kinds of investigation which draw on similar materials. In *Mirage in the West*, Durand Echeverria has analyzed the French image of the United States in an effort to improve international understanding and cooperation. A far more common approach has been the examination of Americans appearing in foreign plays and novels as a means of measuring the impact of tourism and national policy; the viewpoint is American and the question, often, Do they like us? A third type of study has described the echoes of an author's American visit that later appear in his work. I have found all three kinds of material useful, the first for background, the second as an index to materials which occasionally proved worthy of careful study, and the third as often directly to the purpose when the artist had successfully assimilated his material and thus escaped mere local color. This supportive research is recorded in my notes and in the initial essay.

My efforts to examine the role America has been made to play in a few serious books has led me inevitably to a critical assessment of the literature itself. For the most part I have limited my illustrations to writing I have found critically interesting; the amount of space allotted is a rough indication of my preferences. Although I have taken its imaginative uses as a focal point, the general discussion of the American metaphor has not shaped my choice of books. I have been guided by what is aesthetically, creatively of the highest quality; that is, starting as a question in aesthetics, my book has taken the shape of an exegetical exercise couched in cultural-historical terms.

My effort to understand these books rests on an important assumption. I do not deny for a moment the contribution of the unconscious, the muse, or the Holy Spirit to the creation of art. But these things are notoriously difficult to explain—short of psychology or mystic intuition. What is decidedly more accessible to the critic is the fruit of his author's talent as distinguished from his genius. One can acknowledge the inspiration of genius, I think, and yet for purposes of criticism regard literature largely as artifact, the concrete evidence of problems solved and something built. (From this point of view, even the organic might be seen as construction especially successful in its integration and coherence.) My assumption is that the major artist chooses his materials with his ultimate goal more or less clearly in mind and that therefore a firm grasp on any important aspect of a successful work both requires and leads to comprehension of the whole. It is this comprehension that the serious writer demands of us, and it remains the central goal of any book about books.

The emphasis I have been describing can be traced in the Contents listing. After my historical review of Europe's American imagery, I turn in Chapter IV to particular poems, novels, and plays to illustrate what has been done during the twentieth century with this inherited typology. But the more successful a work is in realizing its author's aesthetic purposes, the more it resists categories which press toward simplification and reduction. And so for the final chapter I have selected what seemed important and challenging material and ordered it according to the language of composition. This has ultimately proven least damaging to the work I have been most interested in examining closely, and although I do relatively little with the part played in the writing by the nationality of the author, certain motifs do emerge and lend the discussions coherence—a coherence due finally not only to a common language and political situation but also to the shared literary and cultural legacy that informs the American metaphor I discuss. Since I have been interested for the moment more in art than in history, the sequence of these final discussions implies nothing more than an ascending spiral of creative complexity in the works studied and their use of America.

xiv   *Preface*

"The best parts of the best authors in all languages can be translated," James Russell Lowell argued in 1849. "The key by which we unlock the great galleries of Art is their common human interest. Nature supplies us with lexicon, commentary, and glossary to the great poems of all ages." I tend to agree with Lowell, but the doubts of those who distrust translation suggest caution to the interpreter and limits to the range of his investigation. The present study relies heavily on translations. It touches at one point or another on literature and scholarly commentary in some fifteen languages. Whenever possible, I have examined troublesome phrases in the original; some of the translating was done at my behest and I was able to question passages which seemed crucial. But any use of translation is second-best; I have felt justified here because of the nature of my inquiry. As Auden remarks in his preface to an English rendering of Voznesensky's *Antiworlds,* there are poets like Campion whose metrical and rhythmical music cannot exist outside its original language. But some writers lose less in translation than others. "Even in the crudest prose translation," Auden suggests, "a non-Italian reader can immediately recognize that Dante is a great poet, because much of the impact of his poetry depends upon his use of similes and metaphors drawn from sensory experiences which are not confined to Italians but common to all peoples . . . ." My translations, as far as I can determine, are not crude; each of my discussions has been examined by a professional student of the literature being discussed who reads and speaks the original language. But more to the point, there are few if any Campions discussed here; my concern is with similes, metaphors, and the total statement of novels and plays. When I must work with poetry I have avoided conclusions based on rhythm, rhyme, idiom, or other linguistic features of the work. Each reader must decide for himself whether my larger observations stand where he feels the evidence has been misconceived.

There is yet a further point to be made concerning translations. They do in fact exist for us now as English works, regardless of their relation to their originals. "One of the primary proofs that a poem, or any work of art, has value," Auden adds, "is that, wherever, whenever, and by whomever it was made, we find it relevant to ourselves, our time, and our place. I am certain that Mr. Voznesensky is a good poet because, though I know no Russian and have never been in Russia, his poems, even in English translation, have much to say to me." At the very least, then, this is a book about books important for readers of English.

R.R.

Washington University
St. Louis

Contents

PART ONE

America in Europe's Imagination
Notes toward the Biography of an Image

I

The Invention of America: I

You're just an image, my dear sir,
just a phantasy, that's all . . . .
—Luigi Pirandello, *Right You Are,*
If You Think You Are

"Did you ever hear of Christopher Columbus?"
"Bien sûr! He invented America; a very great man."
—Henry James, *The American*

James's quip serves nicely to color our attitude toward his coquette, but there is truth in the remark that provides the base on which the essays of Part Two rest. In those discussions I try to show how serious artists have made metaphoric use of the concept of America provided them by their culture. Here I would like to trace briefly the history of the concept they inherited, the significant moments in the growth of the image we will see employed in the central portion of this book. (And I want to provide the fullest bibliographic annotation I can. Much of what follows is familiar to students of American-European cultural relations, and yet I know of no bibliography or introduction to the subject which might lead a new inquirer quickly to the large mass of material already available on his subject.)

As with everything else in the present book, that subject has little to do with the actual United States; the scholar or scholars who undertake its thorough examination must acknowledge that what men believe to be true is, in a sense, true—it will motivate their actions and affect their lives. And their conception of their "truth," if its grip upon them is persistent, will have a history analogous to but separate from the history of men and nations that most agree rests on fact and is therefore in some other sense true.

The idea of America which occupies these pages is one such concept, and it has a history which long antedates the fifteenth century. For, as Edmundo O'Gorman has argued,[1] we should not think of America as having been discovered in 1492. We have discovered something only when we grasp the nature of our find. If we cherish the word *discovery,* we should think in terms of the fifteen years of discussion preceding the *Cosmographia Introductio* of 1507; better yet, because the nature of the new land mass was actually projected on it by the European mind, America was *invented*—not by Columbus, but perhaps by Vespucci. More accurately, it was constructed gradually as the imagination of the Old World found a congenial definition for the New. And although I shall try to argue that the process shows signs of completion, my book is based on the assumption that Europe has been building its image of America at least since 1492. Indeed, if the myths of classic antiquity are seen as the anticipations they are, America was invented long before Columbus set sail.

There is a Babylonian tablet of the fifth century B.C., in the British Museum, believed to be the oldest extant cartographical document. It depicts the world as an island surrounded by water. Homer held a similar view, speaking of a northern and a southern part; by the time of Ptolemy, the ancients had agreed on an earth of three parts: Europe, Asia, and Africa. This was the *orbis terrarum* inherited by the Renaissance. The ancients had been willing to conceive in addition the possibility of an *orbis alterius,* probably at the antipodes, and as pagans they had no reason to doubt that these other lands might be inhabited. Christians, however, were committed to the unity of all mankind through descent from Adam and Eve. They could not include in their world-view men who had not had an opportunity to hear the gospel or share in Christ's redemption. St. Augustine flatly denied the existence of antipodal land.

When Columbus set out he hoped by sailing west to reach the

eastern edge of the Island of Earth. As far as we know, he never came to doubt that he had done so. Others, like his Spanish patrons and the scholar Peter Martyr, had reservations. But the questions that would have to be faced if Columbus's interpretation of his adventure were mistaken were distressingly fundamental: they touched the very nature of the Creation and man's relationship to it. When Columbus began to suspect the size of the land mass which he encountered on his third voyage, he turned once again to a priori reasoning: it was quite possible, he wrote, that he was near Eden, or at least in a fresh-water gulf fed by a fountain in the Terrestrial Paradise. Amerigo Vespucci, however, based his hypothesis on what he had in fact seen. When his long journey down the eastern coast of South America convinced him both that he was not near Asia and that this land could not adjoin the *orbis terrarum*, Vespucci began to think along the lines taken in his famous letter, "A New World" *(Mundus Novus,* 1503). The difficult idea from the point of view of Christian Europe was not that these lands might be "new"; the challenge was to accept them as both new and *inhabited.* If the natives Columbus and others had met did not live on or near the traditional *orbis terrarum,* all the initial questions had to be faced. Neither Vespucci nor his contemporaries could satisfy themselves as to where these men originated (the existence of something like the Bering Strait was hypothesized very early), but the gradual agreement that the natives did indeed live in a new part of the *world* had far-reaching implications. What St. Isidore of Seville had postulated many years before was finally and authoritatively affirmed in the *Cosmographia Introductio* and the accompanying maps of Martin Waldseemuller (1507). The habitable world has not three but four parts, ". . . and the first three parts are continents, the fourth is an island."

This uncommon use of "continent" is meant to suggest "contiguous" to contrast with the new lands, which seemed separate islands. The way was now open to yet another step toward our modern view of the earth. It was not merely new land which had been assimilated to the old *orbis terrarum;* perhaps the greatest imaginative leap of all was to include the ocean. The idea that the world was an island washed by an imprisoning sea yielded to a world of earth punctuated by huge lakes. Thus, eventually, all portions of the world came to be imagined as continental or contiguous. (See the remarkable Ortelius world map of 1587.[2]) "According to the way people are generally made," Nietzsche observed, "the name is what first makes a thing visible." By giving it a name the *Cosmographia Introductio* recognized the independence of America's existence.

Until the question of the new continent's *nature* was settled, however, America could not be said truly to exist. And if we recall Europe's place in the *orbis terrarum,* we will understand why there was no chance whatever that the identity granted America would be truly new or autonomous. From ancient times Europe had claimed the first place in the threefold division of the Island of Earth. The claim was not based on size or wealth, but on the belief that human life began there and continued to be embodied there in its purest form. Later Christian writers accepted European civilization as the best manifestation of natural man and claimed in addition a superiority based on adherence to the only true Church. For an America hesitating at the threshold before occupying its place in the consciousness of the known world, this universally recognized centrality of Europe had far-reaching implications. As Edmundo O'Gorman points out, "European history . . . was not conceived as that of one particular civilization among others, but was lived and felt as the history of the only truly significant culture; European history was universal history. Europe became history's paradigm, and the European way of life came to be regarded as the supreme criterion by which to judge the value and meaning of all other forms of civilization. The spiritual being of the two other parts of the world obviously depended from that of Europe, and so, of course, did the being that was to be attributed to America." In such a view of history, the inhabitants of America could at the very best be seen as natural men deprived of Christian civilization in a land devoid of spiritual meaning. "America was no more than a potentiality, which could be realized only by receiving and fulfilling the values and ideals of European culture. America, in fact, could acquire historical significance only by becoming another Europe. Such was the spiritual or historical being that was invented for America." [3]

The two ways in which Europe sought to remake itself in America are well-enough known, but I want to review them here to help emphasize the nature and scope of the present study. In South America, Europe attempted the direct transplantation of its culture; after the first years of exploration and adjustment, the Spanish and Portuguese were remarkably successful in annexing the new lands as spiritual appendages of the old. This success can be witnessed into the twentieth century, where it has been contested largely by winds blowing from the north. It is the distinctness of the European adventure in North America that justifies my focusing there to the exclusion of Europe's imaginative sense of the south. For in the northern hemisphere the effort was made from the beginning to adapt European culture to the new environment. For the European mind North America early came to seem a new Europe *in the making*. This is what was usually meant by "America"; because both the conception and the name gradually became centered in the north [4] —and for the sake of euphony and conciseness—I have used "America" on most of these pages to mean what came to be the United States.

I have been interested here in establishing Europe's initial invention of America because I have regarded the "America" I discuss in later chapters as a construction of the European imagination. In Chapter II I will try to suggest as succinctly as I can some of the connotations made available to twentieth-century artists by the word *America*. "In the sixteenth and seventeenth centuries, Europeans regarded the Americas as a rich new world. In the eighteenth century, they looked upon America as the home of children of nature, noble redmen and savages, who possessed all the virtues of the human race when uncorrupted by the contaminating influences of civilization and government. In the nineteenth century, the United States became, for many Europeans, the ideal haven of freedom and opportunity, to which men might repair to build a new fatherland." [5] There is a great deal more to the story than this, for ideas rarely sort themselves out so neatly, but these lines from a presidential address to the Mississippi Valley Historical Association will serve to adumbrate the story to come and provide some shape for my remarks.

II

The History of an Image

From Atlantis to a "Rich New World" and the Land of the Noble Savage

> You are not an American with an Indian's broad shoulders and slim waist, with level eyes and a skin tanned by the air of the prairies and the rivers that cross them, you have not been to the Great Lakes and sailed on them, wherever they may be. So, I ask you, what would a pretty girl like me be doing following you?
> —Franz Kafka, *Contemplation*

Once the idea "America" is seen as a construction of the European imagination, it becomes clear that a number of preconceptions were waiting in the wings in 1492 to settle on the newly located, identity-less land mass. One of the oldest was Atlantis, described by Plato in the fourth century B.C. as an island of continental size which had existed some nine thousand years earlier and then disappeared beneath the sea. By Greek standards, the citizens of Atlantis were barbarians. They were descendants of Poseidon and a mortal, and as long as they kept the two sides of their natures in balance they remained beautiful,

9

wealthy and happy. (Apparently, they were, in addition to their other achievements, excellent engineers—as witness the walls, palaces, bridges, and canals described in the *Critias;* dreams of technocracy begin early.) As we have learned to expect, however, divinity cannot hold out for long against ordinary mortal nature. Zeus determined to punish Atlantis and did so with an earthquake that sent the island back to Poseidon.

Plutarch was only one of many later thinkers who took Plato's myth for history; he decided that an island adjoining Atlantis should be called Ogygia (now thought by some to be Greenland), and that there was a great continent a mere five hundred miles to the west. St. Brendan's trip to Scotland and Wales in the sixth century had by the tenth become a fabulous seven-year voyage to the Land Promised to the Saints. In a vision, so the fable goes, Brendan "saw the mighty intolerable ocean on every side and . . . the beautiful noble island, with trains of angels rising from it." He recognized the place as the "fair island" another monk had described to him as rich with "many precious stones shining bright." After the seven-year journey, when the "mist passed away, ... they saw the fairest country . . . that any man might see . . . so clear and bright that it was an heavenly sight to behold; and all the trees were charged with ripe fruit and herbs full of flowers." (On his way to the Land Promised to the Saints, Brendan passed an island where Judas clung precariously to a rock in the raging sea. Dante was later to locate his Purgatorio somewhere in that same fabulous Ocean Sea.[1])

Eldorado, Ultima Thule, Arcadia, the Golden Age—the countless worlds-more-attractive available to Europe—all contributed to the creation of the New World. The basic expectations were common to most of them; these lands are rich and fertile beyond a European's wildest dream, their inhabitants—whether freaks, savages, or gentlemen—are perpetually happy; and society—whether simple or complex—unites men without friction. There was also of course Eden, the Earthly Paradise posited by Columbus to account for his third voyage. Christendom was slow to abandon its search for the actual Garden. When it could not be found in Asia, in India or Ethiopia, many were certain it lay somewhere behind the coastline traced by Columbus, Vespucci, and the other explorers.[2] It takes determined blurring to combine the Eden myth with the earlier pagan stories, blurring reflected in the greed of the conquistadores whose chivalric quest included carrying the word of God to the heathen. Return to the Garden of Eden would seem to promise primarily spiritual riches, or at most a pastoral fecundity to sustain the good Christian in his few quotidian needs. But the sand on the Island of the Seven Cities was believed to be one-third fine gold, and in Atlantis there was "such an amount of wealth as was never before possessed by kings and potentates, and is not likely ever to be again . . . ." Visions such as these provided stern competition for missionary zeal. For centuries Europe has seen America as an enormous mine, the source first of precious metals, then of raw materials, mercantile sales, and the wealthy L'Oncle Sam, *deus ex machina* of many a nineteenth-century French drama. Or, alternatively, the open newness of America combined with classical idealization of the Indian to promise a man-made Eden, from the Utopia of More to the emigrants and political experiments of the nineteenth century to the Baconian technocracy of Stalin's dreams. And if one is willing to combine for a moment the Indian as Apollo Belvidere and the Indian as Child of Satan—two sides of the same myth-making—then there is a clear enough line from the happy savages of Chateaubriand to the violence hymned by Sartre, the violence of Simone de Beauvoir's Chicago and the French cult of Bogart and the American gangster film.[3]

There were those who saw America only in terms of the wealth pictured in explorers' accounts—wealth often more imagined than real, earnestly believed in and described in order to justify present expenditures and future voyages. And there were those whose main concern was the speedy conversion of men heretofore deprived of God's word.[4] (These last often stressed the diabolic savagery of the Indian and rarely talked of the classical Golden Age: their view owes more to the Reformation than to the Renaissance.[5]) But as Gilbert Chinard demonstrates, America occurs most often in the work of serious artists and thinkers as an indictment of the stale and artificial life of Europe. This is the primitivism of

> the French poet Ronsard or ... the story of *El Villano del Danubio* retold by the sixteenth century Spanish writer Antonio de Guevara or even later in Cervantes' description of the Island of Barataria under the rule of good Sancho. To a philosopher like Locke it offered a true image of a condition which had existed before personal property and compacts had laid the foundation of human society such as we know it, for then "all the world was America." But though neither Locke, nor Vico, nor Montesquieu intended to use their praise of the savage as an argument destructive of our form of society, such was clearly the purpose of the Frenchman Lahontan, in his *Dialogues Between an American Savage and the Author* (1703), and to a lesser extent of Jean-Jacques Rousseau.

"Whether they intended it or not," Chinard concludes, "these advocates of a more or less complete return to nature were the forerunners of some of our modern anarchists and communistic utopians .... America as an idea was already at work pointing the way in the never-ending and hitherto chimerical quest of happiness." [6]

"This discovery of a boundless country seems worthy of consideration," Montaigne wrote about 1580.[7] His consideration occupies some ten pages in the famous "Of Cannibals" and three or four more in "Of Coaches" (*c.* 1585); it became one of the most influential pictures of American life ever drawn. Montaigne is less concerned with the boundless country than the primitive life lived there, but his real subject is the contrast between native and European. The Indians seem barbaric merely because they are different, he notes; they "are wild, just as we call wild the fruits that nature has produced by herself and in her normal course ...."[8]

> These nations ... seem to be barbarous in this sense, that they have been fashioned very little by the human mind, and

are still very close to their original naturalness. The laws of nature still rule them, very little corrupted by ours; and they are in such a state of purity that I am sometimes vexed that they were unknown earlier, in the days when there were men able to judge them better than we. I am sorry that Lycurgus and Plato did not know of them; for it seems to me that what we actually see in these nations surpasses not only all the pictures in which poets have idealized the golden age and all their inventions in imagining a happy state of man, but also the conceptions and the very desire of philosophy. They could not imagine a naturalness so pure and simple as we see by experience; nor could they believe that our society could be maintained with so little artifice and human solder. This is a nation, I should say to Plato, in which there is no sort of traffic, no knowledge of letters, no science of numbers, no name for a magistrate or for political superiority, no custom of servitude, no riches or poverty, no contracts, no successions, no partitions, no occupations but leisure ones, no care for any but common kinship, no clothes, no agriculture, no metal, no use of wine or wheat. The very words that signify lying, treachery, dissimulation, avarice, envy, belittling, pardon—unheard of. How far from this perfection would he find the republic that he imagined: *Men fresh sprung from the gods* [Seneca].

These manners nature first ordained.
Virgil [9]

Such men with such manners live an enviable life indeed: "The whole day is spent in dancing." [10]

The reference to classical writers and the Golden Age suggests the standard with which Montaigne judges contemporary France. Indian verse, he decides, is Anacreontic, and their language "is a soft language, with an agreeable sound, somewhat like Greek in its endings." [11] If only the Greeks or Romans had come to this land, their virtues would have been fit additions to the fine natural beginnings of the natives. But while "it was still quite naked at the breast, and lived only on what its nursing mother provided," [12] this new world tasted corruption and exploitation. As a young world, it will live on after the old has fallen into paralysis,[13] but it will always bear the scars of Europe's greed. "We took advantage of their ignorance and inexperience to incline them the more easily toward treachery, lewdness, avarice, and every sort of inhumanity and cruelty, after the example and pattern of our ways. Who ever set the utility of commerce and trading at such a price? So many cities razed, so many nations exterminated, so many millions of people put to the sword, and the richest and most beautiful part of the world turned upside down, for the traffic in pearls and pepper!" [14] That some natives are cannibals Montaigne does not deny, but since his target is contemporary European life, his Indians remain essentially noble and Greek until spoiled by contact with the invader from the east. The manipulation becomes in itself a tradition; Montaigne is an ancestor of the twentieth-century artist who chooses America to mirror European deficiencies.

 Montaigne's America shared the popularity of his *Essays.* There is a copy of Florio's 1603 translation in the British Museum bearing Shakespeare's autograph, the only book known for certain to have belonged to the dramatist. By 1610, when *The Tempest* was written, Shakespeare found Montaigne's images and language sufficiently apt to quote directly in the first scene of Act II. In the mouth of Gonzalo, however, Montaigne's primitivism seems an attractive but naïve fantasy: "Prithee, no more," cries Alonso, "thou dost talk nothing to me"—even Gonzalo eventually admits that his vision is merely "merry fooling." Shakespeare uses the familiar Montaigne material as a starting point, as an introduction to his examination of Caliban and Prospero, the amorality of the primitive and the superiority of full moral consciousness. But even Shakespeare's parody cannot destroy the charm of Montaigne's imagery: "O brave new world," cries Miranda, "that has such people in't!" [15]

    The genesis of *The Tempest* is customarily seen in the shipwreck off Bermuda of the ship *Sea Adventure* which had sailed for Virginia in 1609. The detailed descriptions of this event were certainly made widely available to public curiosity, for tales from America always aroused interest and often found their way into the work of Elizabethan writers. For Marlowe and many another author, "rich America" was simply the source of Spanish wealth and a challenge to British enterprise. "Is there such treasure there, captain, as I have heard?" asks a character contributed by Chapman to Jonson and Marston's *Eastward Ho!* "I tell thee," comes the reply, "gold is more plentiful there than copper is with us; and for as much red copper as I can bring, I'll have thrice the weight in gold. Why, man, all their dripping pans and their chamber pots are pure gold . . . ; and for rubies and diamonds they go forth on holidays and gather 'em by the sea shore." [16] Green, Peele, Lyly, Massinger, Chapman, or Shakespeare—any one might be the author of Marlowe's lines in *Tamburlane:*

> Desire of gold, great sir?
> That's to be gotten in the Western Ind.

Spenser chides his countrymen for their lack of enterprise in letting Spain win her way to European ascendancy; England has failed

> in conquest of that land of gold.
> But this to you, O Britons, most pertains
> To whom the right hereof itself hath sold,
> To which, for sparing little cost or pains
> Lose so immortal glory and so endless gains.

Spenser's reference to the New World reaches beyond this, however, for he uses it to lend substance to his fairyland:

> . . . none that breatheth living aire, does know
> Where is that happy land of Faery
> Which I so much doe vaunt, yet no where show.
> ....
>
> But let that man with better sence advize
> That of the world least part to us is red:
> And daily how through hardy enterprize
> Many great Regions are discovered,

Which to late age were never mentioned.
Who ever heard of th' Indian Peru?
Or who in venturous vessell measured
The Amazons huge river, now found trew?
Or fruitfullest Virginia who did ever vew?

Yet all these were when no man did them know,
Yet have from wisest ages hidden beene:
....

Of Faery Land yet if he more inquyre,
By certein signes, here sett in sondrie place,
He may it fynd.[17]

The epigraph at the beginning of this volume attests to the
inspired imagery of Donne's love poems: he is able to raise a more
philosophical matter (and recall Montaigne) through reference to

That unripe side of earth, that heavy clime
That gives us man up now, like Adam's time
Before he ate . . . .

Virginia, wrote Michael Drayton in 1606, is earth's "onely paradise." In 1577 appeared *Joyfull Newes Out of the Newe Founde World,*
a translation from the Spanish of Nicholas Monardes, "treatying
of the singular and rare vertues of certain Hearbes, Trees, Oyles,
Plantes, Stones, and Drugges of the West Indias." [18] Everyone
naturally assumed that the fruits of Fairyland, of Paradise, would
possess remarkable powers. For John Lyly, the "Nicotian herb"
(tobacco) seemed a sovereign remedy; for many other Elizabethans, the newly imported potato was a welcome aphrodisiac. Alone
with Mistress Ford and Mistress Page in *The Merry Wives of
Windsor,* Falstaff cries, "Let the sky rain potatoes; . . . let there
come a tempest of provocation . . ." (V,v).

In his thorough study of America in Renaissance English literature, Robert Heilman found there was as yet little idealization of the Indian, though there was strong interest in converting
him and building a new Christian commonwealth. In addition,

this new dwelling of the spirit also contained hundreds of products of both sensuous and commercial value, and endless gold of which the glitter filled Europe with mirages of material well-being. There ... were the potentialities of a new golden age marking a return to virtues long stripped from many by vicious society. To reach the scene, intrepid sailors covered vast distances and added a vibration to the thrills evoked by the new land.

... America was an offering of the Renaissance; a new surge of this-worldly interest disclosed new potentialities for life.... A newly curious eye caught America, and its strangeness and fertility gave new impetus to the hopes of a people intensely conscious of the here-and-now.[19]

The French were among the first to see nobility in the Indian: Jodelle's *Ode* anticipated Montaigne by twenty years, and Ronsard joined in condemning European exploration for disturbing the natural simplicity of the savages—a simplicity he had no trouble identifying with the classical Golden Age. But otherwise most of Heilman's conclusions apply as well to DuBellay, DuBartas, and lesser French writers as to the English.[20]

These images can be found in semiofficial guise as late as 1777 in Diderot's *Encyclopédie.* The stories of sea monsters, pygmies, and giant Amazons appear once again, as do accounts of luxuriant natural beauty and great mineral wealth. Despite its publication during the American Revolution, the *Encyclopédie* focuses almost entirely on South America. There is a full-scale examination of Benjamin Franklin—as befits an age of scientific curiosity—but it is the marvel of the unfamiliar, romanticized jungle which continues to dominate the civilized imagination of Europe.[21] How strong this image of America still was became even more clear with the publication and wide circulation of William Bartram's *Travels* (1791) through the Floridas, Carolinas, and Georgia. Bartram's descriptions served Coleridge ("Kubla Khan" and *The Ancient Mariner)* and Wordsworth ("Ruth"), Southey ("Madoc"), Thomas Campbell ("Gertrude of Wyoming," a county in Pennsylvania), and Tennyson *(In Memoriam),* but his influence reached farthest in time and space through his adoption by Chateaubriand.

Buffon had asserted that European flora and fauna degenerated when brought to America (earlier mariners believed that dogs lost their bark). Several visitors had found terror in the forest and Indian cruelty; Goldsmith's *Deserted Village* refers to Georgia as a "dreary scene":

> Those matted woods, where birds forget to sing,
> But silent bats in drowsy clusters cling; . . .
> Where crouching tigers wait their hapless prey,
> And savage men more murderous still than they.[22]

But all such doubts seemed to melt before Chateaubriand's lush heightening of Bartram's details. Rousseau and Bernardin de Saint-Pierre also contributed to *The Natchez, Atala,* and *René,* but it was what Chateaubriand did with this material that brought him fame and took his America into the literature of every European country. His readers not only wept for Atala and René, they believed his portrayal of their environment and the lives the Indians lived there. For after all, had the author not spent five months living with the natives in their blissful state of natural virtue? So at least he claimed. Emma Kate Armstrong concludes her comparison of fact and fancy in Chateaubriand's story of the visit with nice irony: "A careful examination of Chateaubriand's works shows that two of his statements . . . may be accepted without hesitation: he came to Baltimore, and his letter of introduction from the Marquis de la Rouërie was received by Washington." [23]

What Chateaubriand did and what he saw in 1791 is of very little importance; he said he saw a great deal and Europe felt the truth of his fables. He had come with a fantastic dream of locating the Northwest Passage singlehandedly; he abandoned this scheme but left with plans for *The Natchez,* "an epic of the natural man." This tribute to the heroic Red Indian was not published until 1826, but two episodes originally prepared for it appeared much earlier. In his use of America in *Atala* and *René,* Chateaubriand invites the kind of study I pursue in later portions of this book. His fantastic setting is used to provide a moral challenge for his central characters, and the two stories emerge as simple para-

bles celebrating orthodox Christianity. It is significant that Chateaubriand decided to attach *Atala* and *René* to his sentimental
return to the faith, *The Spirit of Christianity* (1802), for *Atala* does
demonstrate "the harmonies of the Christian religion with the
scenes of nature and the passions of the human heart" as its
author hoped, and even *René* can be read as testimony to the
healing power of religious belief. Such a reading in no way accounts for the enormous popularity of the two stories, however.
Atala went through seven German editions by 1825; it would take
a separate volume to indicate the writers who have felt the force of
its influence in one way or another.

In one sense, Chateaubriand's America might be seen as a
culmination of the image-making that began in the classical
fables; in another sense it helped focus those traditional elements
that were taking new shape as the romantic movement. Here is
one witness to the force of Chateaubriand's image; he writes in
1960, but this should only illustrate how durable a fascinating
image can be. Chateaubriand, according to Raymond Lebègue,
was able to combine ". . . a precise evocation of the American
landscape and of Indian life, an exoticism which, while remaining
accessible to the reader, gave him the illusion of living in the New
World, descriptions rivaling those of the plastic arts, a verbal
music never heard before, ideas of the real world . . . ." [24] For
many years, M. Lebègue concludes, this was the only America the
French knew.

Moreover, "Chateaubriand prepared the French to read the
Indian stories of Fenimore Cooper." Cooper's immense popularity in Europe can best be understood as participating in the
Chateaubriand tradition. (Among later French writers, Balzac,
Hugo, and Dumas père turned occasionally to the same motifs;
when Jules Verne and his brother toured upstate New York, they
addressed each other as Hawkeye and Chingachgook.) "At first
we saw the Indians with Chateaubriand's eyes," Julian Schmidt
remarked in 1871; "then came the series of Cooper's novels." [25]
Gustave Aimard, the French Cooper, wrote more than eighty
western romances between 1843 and 1875; many were translated
into other European languages.[26] His German counterpart, Karl
May, had sold some four million copies of his Old Shatterhand

tales by 1926—and they are still very popular in Germany. Klaus Mann has remarked that May was the favorite author of the young Hitler; May's "childish and criminal fantasia has actually—though obliquely—influenced the history of the world . . . . The third Reich is Karl May's ultimate triumph." [27]

"The Ideal Haven of Freedom and Opportunity"

> Those of our navigators who have studied this half of the Northern American Continent, maintain that an inborn love of liberty inherent to the soil, the sky, forests, and lakes prevents this still young country from resembling the other parts of the Universe. They are convinced that any European transported under this climate will be affected by this particular condition.
> —*Gazette de France* (1774)

One early student of the European idea of America was Alexis de Tocqueville. He planned his visit to America both as an escape from an increasingly inhospitable France and as a possible way up in the world. His ostensible purpose was to study the American prison system for his government, but he was determined from the start to write a book which would win him wide fame in France. A book on America for a French audience, he reasoned, must needs begin with the prejudices, assumptions, and preconceptions of that audience, and so he canvassed his family and friends to discover what they did in fact know and believe about

the United States. As it turned out, France itself became the
implicit center of *Democracy in America* (1835, 1840). Curiosity
about America played its part in bringing Tocqueville here for
nine months in 1831, and similar curiosity prompted his book and
assured its success. But the America of the *Democracy* is basically a
model for Tocqueville's investigation of social, legal, and economic equality and its effects. Like many another nineteenth-
century observer, Tocqueville believed that the force of this
equality would eventually be felt everywhere. Thus the whole
world should be interested in the most advanced case of democratic leveling available for study: "I avow that in America, I
have seen more than America."

Interest in America during the late eighteenth and the nineteenth centuries ran higher than at any time since the Renaissance. The Revolutionary War (guerre de l'Amérique) and the
coincident social, economic, and political upheavals of the next
hundred years in Europe revived earlier utopian dreams and
prompted wave after wave of emigration. "God help America to
fight its way to liberty," cried a Norwegian clergyman in 1781, so
"that mankind may not perish in serfdom." [28] There were many
in Europe to agree with the remark of Benjamin Franklin's friend,
Dr. Richard Price: "Perhaps I do not go too far, when I say that,
next to the introduction of Christianity among mankind, the
American Revolution may prove the most important step in the
progressive course of human improvement." The roots of our
Revolution in Montesquieu and Rousseau should not obscure the
influence of the American on the French conflagration. Indeed, as
Lamartine remarked nearly a hundred years later, "One would
need the discernment of God himself to distinguish America from
France after their respective causes had been fused together during and after the American Revolutionary War." For Germany
and Italy as well, America emerged for the first time as a political
force—and, for many, a challenging alternative. In addition, the
image of America gained those two clusters of suggestion, George
Washington and Benjamin Franklin. Whenever military courage
and selfless service to the commonwealth was the subject—as, for
instance, to berate Napoleon or his imperial descendants through
Mussolini and Hitler—the name of Washington might be in-

voked, "the first—the last—the best—/ The Cincinnatus of the West." Franklin's image is richer. He suggested to Europe the poise and simple grace of the exceptionally successful diplomat, but his manner and his republican freedom from pretension has been less important to the American metaphor than his reputation for scientific achievement. Here later history has contributed to selective heightening of the man's original impact: industrial development and scientific advance have witnessed the truth of the sorcery and Promethean daring of Franklin, Edison, and the American heroes of Jules Verne.

France, England, and Spain had produced a library of observation and commentary on America by the beginning of the nineteenth century; these images were imported by Italy and Russia and remained virtually unchanged before the beginning of the modern era. Until the late eighteenth century, Germany too relied upon her western neighbors for a picture of America, but then the Revolution sparked a journalistic enthusiasm which fed in turn several decades of historical, scientific, and literary activity. Since interest in the United States after the wars of 1776 and 1812 was so widespread in Europe, I cannot begin to touch its limits here; moreover, little was added to the images we have traced before they passed into the hands of the modern artist.[29] Germany's image of America in the nineteenth century is worth examining, however, both because of its later literary influence and because of its contemporary effect on emigration. "Ah, let me but stand securely on American soil, where all is new," cries the hero of Klinger's *Storm and Stress* (1775). The date is significant. Elsewhere in Europe the idea had been amply explored, but under the impulse of the Revolution it came alive in Germany with fresh vigor and gained momentum for its entry into the twentieth century.

As Biedermann remarked, "With the war for independence the educated classes in Germany begin for the first time to turn toward America." Kant, Schiller, Herder, Wieland, Schubert, Klopstock, Gleim—"Our men of learning and our poets," Robert Pruz noted in 1843, "believed that there were ideas here at work very similar to those so often dreamed of: all men brethren,

heaven on earth, and Astraea in person mistress of the new Utopia." The force of Washington and Franklin reached Germany
—Franklin had visited in 1776—and the stream of German mer-
cenaries who participated made the war a personal matter for
many Germans. This early enthusiasm for America was short-
lived, however. Dietrich von Bülow's influential *The Free State of
North America in Its Latest Development* (1797) records his disenchantment after two visits to America (he lost his fortune specu-
lating in American land in 1796); the selling of soldiers had never
been popular and most Germans resisted and resented it; and the
French Revolution washed over German enthusiasm for the
American war like a cold shower.[30] I shall discuss the mature
Goethe's idea of America in a moment. Here it is sufficient to note
that he and Schiller were the only two major classical writers to
make occasional comment on America. The early Romantic
writers rarely escaped their preoccupation with aesthetics. Dorothea Veit's *Florentin* (1801) proposes America as an arena for
European adventurers, and Jean Paul suggested it as the fountain
of youth for weary European intellectuals, but Tieck feared what
appeared to him the industrial spirit of Americans. Novalis sums
this early detachment nicely and turns America into metaphor in
his now-famous phase: "America is here or nowhere." [31] The
current intellectual renaissance was, he felt, a more significant
human achievement than the discovery of America.

Some time about 1815, however, German Romanticism turned
to America as an example of the model commonwealth. Platen,
Grün, Freiligrath, Ludwig, Chamisso, Follen, Gall, Duden, Lenau
—all, at one time or another,

> ... pictured it in highly imaginative style as a new and
> youthful world in contrast with the dying culture of Europe.
> Thus the romantic conception of America won its dominant
> position in German literature and, although strongly at-
> tacked from time to time, maintained this place until late in
> the nineteenth century. In the unreal light of this conception
> America appeared, first of all, as a land where nature had
> lost none of her primitive forces, with mighty streams and
> exotic forests, with virgin soil and exuberant vegetation.

Furthermore, the Romantic writers viewed the Western Republic as a refuge from political and economic depression in
Germany and from European weariness in general. They
extolled America as the land of political and civic liberty and
firmly believed that the New World was the promised land, a
new Eden, destined to become the scene of mankind's future
civilization.[32]

With the exception of the idealized Indian, none of these Romantic images can be found in German writing on the New
World between 1776 and 1800.[33] But then von Humboldt's accounts of his travels in America from 1799 to 1804 were reinforced
by the imported imagery of Chateaubriand, Irving, and Cooper,
and the consequent pictures became standard even for authors
not wholly sympathetic toward American life.

"America, you have it better," Goethe wrote in 1827. We may
make what we will of his assertion that he would sail for America
if he were twenty years younger, but the fact remains that his
counterpart in *Wilhelm Meister's Travels* (1821, 1829) does precisely that. He leads his company of migrants to America, to a
new world Goethe seems certain will bring them the spiritual
release, the mobility, the arena for collective, concrete action they
seek. Goethe records that he read again and again a claim in the
Edinburgh Review that "There is nothing to awaken fancy in that
land of dull reality, it contains no objects that carry back the
mind to the contemplation of early antiquity; no mouldering
ruins to excite curiosity in the history of past ages." His preoccupation with America in his later years grew from his inversion of
the usual European complaint that America was hopelessly raw
and naked of civilization. It was this very freshness which attracted him; it was what he associated with an imagined freedom
from old bedrock ("keine Basalte") in his famous little poem.

Goethe's extraordinary curiosity and range brought him to
every source of information on America available in his Germany.
But nothing fired his imagination like the novels of Cooper. He
read them with delight and with remarkable care, and when he
made a survey of contemporary writing in 1827, he challenged
the highest talents of his time to compete with the genius of
Cooper. The subject lay waiting: the heretofore neglected history

and geographic sweep of America. And once the setting is determined, what would be better than a Moses leading his people to
the Promised Land? Goethe reveals that he is himself investigat-
ing the possibilities here and will keep working on his recipe until
he is satisfied with it.[34]

Preston A. Barba was among the first modern scholars to discuss Goethe's plans for an emigrant novel. As Barba remarked in
1914, the influence of Cooper was effectually reinforced for both
the German writer and his public by the growing flood of European migrants crossing the Atlantic. By 1817 twenty thousand
Germans had left for America. In ten years fifteen thousand more
followed, and between 1831 and 1840 the figure rose to nearly
150,000.[35] The United States census of 1850 reported 400,000
German immigrants during the preceding decade, and in 1860 it
counted 950,000 more.[36] Thus Goethe's idea for an American
novel points as much to an examination of the emigrant German
as it does to the adventure tales of Karl May.

Although later efforts toward realism occasionally question the
promise of better life in America, all this writing must be counted
among the strong forces encouraging emigration. The local-color
methods of Scott and the "factual" narratives of earlier emigrants
were grafted onto the preconceptions of the Romantics; the result
was a seemingly endless stream of books and poems which now
read like guides to relocation:

> Spindler describes New York and its neighboring country in
> colonial days; Biernatzki presents the social conditions of the
> slaves on southern plantations; Gerstäcker leads us to the
> adventurers and settlers in Arkansas, Ohio, and Louisiana
> and to the gold-diggers in California; Auerbach shows us the
> independence and prosperity of German immigrants on
> their farms in the Middle West; Grün, Hoffman von Fal-
> lersleben, and Schults describe in detail American pioneer
> life on the Ohio and Mississippi, in Texas and Wisconsin.
> Willkomm portrays the character of the American in all its
> straightforward simplicity.[37]

None of these dealt as often or as fully with America as did
Charles Sealsfield, and none could have had quite the influence

his stories did on the vast numbers of Germans who left Germany for America. Sealsfield

> paints the grandeur and majesty of the American landscape in Louisiana, Pennsylvania, and Texas, the picturesque variety of a scene in New York harbor, or the beauties of the Indian summer along the Hudson. We admire the marvelous pioneer work of American settlers in conquering the wilderness for civilization. We become acquainted with many and various types of Americans in the earlier decades of the century. We hear of glorious deeds and great statesmen in American history from the Revolutionary War to the struggle of the Texans for independence from Mexico, [of city] and country life in their different aspects, the American form of government with its advantages and weaknesses, American culture and American industry, the difficult problem of slavery, economic and social conditions in the older States and among the settlers on the frontier . . . .[38]

A history of American immigration would have to begin with the earliest efforts at colonization and touch upon the Protestant refugees of the Thirty Years' War and the Counter-Reformation and the Puritan settlers of the seventeenth century. It is even possible, with whimsical hindsight, to see Milton's Mammon "as a kind of American angel, full of the pioneer spirit." [39] But it was not until the nineteenth century that immigration became a mass movement. The revolution added the promise of civil liberty to earlier images of wealth, and when economic and political upheaval struck Ireland, Germany, and Italy, America became the goal of hundreds of thousands for whom Europe represented only serfdom. "It is not enough," Condorcet had said, "that the rights of man be written in the books of philosophers and inscribed in the hearts of virtuous men; the weak and ignorant must be able to read them in the example of a great nation. America has given us that example." Every possible appeal America might possess was made in the voluminuous literature promoting emigration,[40] but Emma Lazarus caught most of it in her brief inscriptions for the image of liberty conceived by Laboulaye and Bartholdi for New York harbor:

Give me your tired, your poor,
Your huddled masses yearning to breathe free,
The wretched refuse of your teeming shore.
Send these, the homeless, tempest-tost to me,
I lift my lamp beside the golden door.

By midcentury there were probably few who believed that the golden door would lead everyone to the wealth of the Incas, but they were confident, one and all, that they would have—in Bishop Berkeley's words—"shoes on their feet, cloaths on their backs, and beef in their bellies." [41]

For the philosophers referred to by Condorcet there was yet another element in the imagined promise of life in America. The man of education, the aristocrat, and the poet had long played with the idea of a perfect commonwealth. Like Paradise, it was doubtless to be found Nowhere, but unlike Paradise, the perfections of Utopia might well be man-made—could certainly be made by man if he learned to use his head and control his instincts. In the constructions of Plato, of Bacon and More, the game was played largely in the mind for the pleasure of the conception, or perhaps as an indictment of a world so far inferior to what man might imagine. But from the first America inspired utopian dreams of quite another sort. As the Jesuit communities in South America and the northern experiments from New England to California indicate, America has repeatedly seemed the very Nowhere dreamt of in Europe's philosophy. In 1734 Voltaire wrote that the Golden Age was not merely a dream of poets but did in fact exist in Pennsylvania. For the Marquis de Lezay-Marnesia, who tried to found a refuge for French aristocrats in 1790 at Pittsburgh, America seemed "a world where earth, principles, and man move together in a natural and tranquil liberty, illumined by the fear of God." [42] Coleridge and Southey planned to establish their Pantisocracy in America, and Madame de Staël thought for a while of moving her salon here. America

was the land where Robert Owen after his unsuccessful experiment in England came to build his New Harmony and where the German Rapp established his communistic village

of Economy, sixteen miles from Pittsburgh. The Napoleonic
exiles, after Waterloo, had come as "soldier farmers" with
General Bertrand to plant "the vine and the olive" in the
wilds of Texas and Alabama. It was known that, while the
theories of Fourier could not be put to the test of experience
in Europe, a group of New England writers managed to
conduct a famous if inconclusive experiment at Brook Farm.
America was the only country on earth where the French
socialist Cabet could attempt to organize colonies of Icar-
ians, because nowhere else could small groups, advocates
of a new order, establish and govern themselves locally
and practically without any interference from a central
government.[43]

As late as 1876 Count Charles Chlapowski and his wife, the
Shakespearean actress Helena Modjeska, became enthusiastic
over the possibility of a Polish utopia; Henryk Sienkiewicz joined
their group and preceded it to southern California. (The experiment began with eight members but soon dissolved.) In her *Mem-
oirs,* Madame Modjeska recalled her earlier expectations—not, I
should guess, without some pleasure in her own credulity: "Oh,
but to cook under the sapphire-blue sky in the land of Freedom!
What joy! To bleach linen at the brook like the maidens of
Homer's *Iliad!* After the day of toil, to play the guitar and sing by
moonlight, to recite poems, or to listen to the mockingbird! and
listening to our songs would be charming Indian maidens, our
neighbors, making wreaths of luxuriant wild flowers for us! And
in exchange we should give them trinkets for their handsome
brown necks and wrists!" [44]

For the individual as well as the group America had long
seemed the home of peace and blessed independence. The list of
political exiles is lengthy—Comte de Noailles, Tallyrand, Volney,
Jerome Bonaparte, Achille Murat. When Schiller went into hiding, he sought to conceal his whereabouts by inventing two letters
to friends which declared his intention of fleeing to America.
Stendhal came to despise American commercialism and ignorance, but early in his life he was an ardent supporter of the
republicanism he identified with America, "the most acceptable

government there is." [45] In 1805 and 1806 he even talked of emigration. Heinrich Heine also considered moving to America, as did Leopold von Gockingk—although apparently not for political reasons. "His wife, he complained, . . . was always sick and depressed and he was getting old and grey before his time, working only for others. 'I should rather work for myself, go to Pennsylvania, and make arable some mountain top with a sweeping view,' he wrote." [46] Nikolaus Lenau, the brooding poet of nightmare, delusion, and *Weltschmerz,* actually did flee to America, the "paradise of freedom" in search of adventure, fortune, and poetic inspiration—and to escape, one student suggests, a romantic entanglement at home. "I want to send my imagination to school in the North American primeval forests," Lenau wrote to his brother-in-law.

> I want to hear the roaring of the Niagara . . . . In America nature is more beautiful and majestic than in Europe. . . . I expect a wonderful effect from it on my mind. In the New World, perhaps a new world of poetry will arise in me. I truly feel something slumbering in me, quite different from what I have been till now. Perhaps this unknown will be awakened by the thundering of the Niagara! How beautiful in itself is the name Niagara! Niagara! Niagara!

He visited Niagara, bought four hundred acres of land, and lived for a time with the Rappists in Economy, Pennsylvania. But he was not happy. He disliked his isolation and neither his physical nor his mental health suited him to the life of a pioneer. His early raptures had drawn on literary convention and so did his rejection: he substituted one myth for another. He found neither nightingales nor good wine, and when he returned home he insisted that birds had no song and flowers no smell in America; for him America became a private symbol of annihilation.[47]

Perhaps the most virulent attack on Europe's myth of America was Ferdinand Kürnberger's *I Am Tired of America* (1856)—it ends with the assertion that all the world will one day be German. Kürnberger's tirade is an implicit response to Ernest Willkomm's *We Are Tired of Europe* (1838), but the earlier book retained its popularity and influence and inspired a persistent stream of hopeful emigrant fiction. Similarly, Hegel's view that "America is . . . the land of the future, . . . the land of desire for all those who are weary of the historical lumber-room of Europe" remained more typical than Tieck's complaint that the industrial ugliness of Fürth was an instance of Americanism.[48]

"Tragic, Cruel, and Sublime"—The Future of Civilization

> It is, after all, a continent ill-tamed by man, a land violated rather than espoused, a land which, under the brutal knee, one still senses as savage, refractory, irreducible. The poets have known it well: another world, not entirely authentic, divided by a double nostalgia of memory of the East and curiosity for the West. It breathes an atmosphere of suspense, of the day's end, impregnated in the North with a puritan melancholy (the novels of Hawthorne), in the South with a stagnant stupor, funereal, mortuary (the marshes of Carolina, the cypresses under their floating shrouds of Spanish moss, the poems of Edgar Allan Poe, the novels of Caldwell and Faulkner). And within is the continual presence, surrounding and penetrant, of an autochthonous fluid, an electricity now raising you up, surfeiting, overexciting you to the point of hysteria, then leaving you helpless, defunct, annihilated . . . . Strangers: there are only strangers here. *Exile.* Quickly now, alcohol, gin, politics, dancing, the movies, the automobile, and from the automobile, like the signal of a shipwrecked man, an antenna desperately hoisted!
>
> —Paul Claudel, "A Poem by St.-John Perse"

The writers discussed in the central portion of this book attest to the durability of Europe's imagined America. They have, moreover, all played their part in supplementing and reinforcing the imagery they inherited. But since my later remarks on the present century focus on their *use* of this imagery, I want to conclude the present historical and bibliographical survey with a brief summary of the connotations America tended to suggest to Europeans during the first half of the twentieth century.

The years since 1492 brought Europe a great many facts about America, but the earlier imagery remained remarkably intact. The vivid experience of exploration, colonization, and immigration seems to have altered Europe's initial expectations hardly at all: with allowance for the rise and fall of political accident, America has continued to carry many of the connotations for the modern European that his countrymen shared earlier. The following citations, embodying as they do quite distinct points of view, should help illustrate the point.

In 1959 the Spring issue of *Italian Quarterly* was devoted entirely to an examination of cultural relations between Italy and the United States. The journal's editor, Carlo L. Golino, contributed an essay, "On the Italian 'Myth' of America," which begins:

> Some of the more singular pages in Carlo Levi's *Christ Stopped at Eboli* deal with the description of Southern peasants' ideas about America. Along with the traditional and inevitable concept of America as the land with streets paved in gold, we sense in these peasants a truly deep attachment for a land which, after all, they know only by hearsay. So intense, in fact, is their devotion and so strong their affection for America, this strange and distant land, that they seem tied to it by bonds stronger than the tenuous ones that link them with the capital of their own country, Rome. This vision of America, for it is a vision, has little correspondence with reality, but it is nevertheless an active force, for it looms on the horizon as a possible, though improbable, Mecca. A product of their individual and collective imagination, this vision is the promised land of which every generation of men

has dreamed, and which for this particular group of peasants in this particular place and time, is called America. Like all myths it is never well defined. Rather, its deepest lure comes from its very nebulosity, never fully penetrated and never completely materialized, and which potentially and ever-lastingly holds the key to the deliverance from the harsh and cruel life of Southern Italy.

Golino remarks that one aspect or another of this myth has appealed to every level of Italian society, that its attraction has not been confined to the southern peasantry. It has flourished in Italy for discernible historical reasons: there were fewer nine-teenth-century travelers to America from Italy than from most European countries, and the struggle for independence in 1870 and the problems encountered in unifying a heterogeneous pop-ulace limited foreign contact even further. America long played its part as a distant, shining example of political freedom, but it was not until the shortcomings of the new Italy became apparent that America came to seem a tempting alternative. As Golino notes, "The very inability of the new Italian nation to assimilate the South into its economic structure led to the mass migrations characteristic of the last decade of the past century, which mark for the first time a massive contact between Italy and the United States."

Golino complains of the inaccuracies which characterize Italy's myth of America. His essay traces to the Second World War what he regards as a self-indulgent construction, and it ends with doubt that the myth will ever be totally dispelled—although he sees reason to rejoice in recent evidence of a "more solidly grounded opinion of America." Since Golino's ideal is accuracy in interna-tional imagery, he tends to criticize those who have participated in myth-making. He complains that little in the way of precise reporting could be expected from the hundreds of thousands who emigrated between 1880 and 1910. Most were young, and they sailed for America so soon after unification that they had no sense of Italian nationality. "These emigrants left Italy as Neapolitans, Sicilians, Calabrians and not as Italians, and continued to consider themselves as such for the rest of their lives." Their ignorance kept them far from the center of American life, but what they did come to understand was never made available to the emerging Italian consciousness: it was filtered back to their former homes and dissipated in unverified half-truth.

America's technical efficiency was warmly welcomed when she entered the First World War; D'Annunzio's "All' America in armi" (1918), was a typical paean to the military might of the savior of the world. With fascism, however, came a new, official image, decadent democracy, and then, by way of reaction, "the most fruitful myth of America"—fruitful, for Golino, because this myth "was the incentive that led, after the last war, to a greater understanding of America, or at least to a much better and more accurate knowledge of it."

Two men in particular were responsible for what amounted to a true cult of America. Both were anti-fascist and both were writers. In the last few years their names, Elio Vittorini and Cesare Pavese, have become quite familiar to American readers, but their role as disseminators of American literature and culture in Italy in the thirties is still not fully acknowledged. To these two men and to a large number of Italian intellectuals who could barely manage to breathe the stifling air of fascist Italy, America became, as it had been for the penniless emigrant of the previous generation, the promised land, the land of freedom, the land where human dignity still prevailed. Under the circumstances America became for these men a kind of forbidden fruit. In a clandestine atmosphere they created a vision of America in direct opposition to the notion of "decadent democracy" imposed from above. The majority were men of letters, hence their interest focused primarily upon American literature. In this way they were fortunate because the fascist censor would be more favorably inclined toward literary criticism than toward political theorizing or economic investigations concerning the United States.

Golino credits this generation of literary critics with beginning a study of America which may one day yield "a much better and accurate knowledge of it." Nevertheless, their vision was "far . . . from the truth"; it "corresponded not so much to reality as to the spiritual and intellectual needs of their own lives." This America was "a vigorous and vital civilization, often untamed and at times tinged with brutality, but always human and humane, carrying in its forward progress most of the answers to mankind's problems. The more the fortunes of fascism and nazism were in the ascendant the more these persecuted men attributed to America all those ideas they saw lacking around them." This was, as Golino remarks, wishful thinking, and while it led some to America it led others to communism—and many to a blurred confusion of the two. Golino is interested in political realities and argues energetically against diluting them with illusions. He moves from illiterate immigrants to Soldati's impressionist *America, My First Love;* from the surface journalism of Ojetti's *America Victorious* and *America and the Future* to the stories of Levi, Alvaro, and Pavese. Each has played its part in the shaping of the myth and so each must share the blame.

In 1947 Howard C. Rice, of the U.S. Information Library in Paris, recalled a French lawyer's response to a luncheon talk Rice had given before a provincial Rotary Club: "You have mentioned American influences in France. . . . Yes, we all know about American machines and American industrial methods. But there are other ways in which America touches us. Perhaps you would like to know how America was gradually revealed to me, a Frenchman who is now in his forties and who has never been to the United States. The first revelation came when I was a boy of ten, in the form of little pamphlets printed in Hamburg, which I bought for a few pennies at the newsstands: the adventures of Buffalo Bill and of Nick Carter. The American West and the city of New York actually lived for me. I had been brought up on the Comtesse de Ségur and the Bibliothèque Rose—and here for the first time I had something else, *action* (though bad literature!) and fresh air! . . . The second revelation was between 1910 and 1920. No, not the American doughboys, though I saw many of them, but the American movies. No movies have ever made such an impression on me since; the westerns but also the Griffiths films, the Gish sisters in "Broken Blossoms" for instance! . . . The third revelation was American jazz: the cake-walk, the blues, and finally Gershwin's *Rhapsody in Blue*. . . ." The lawyer's recollection concludes with praise of Dos Passos, in whose work he found all these things "decanted." In addition to French books, fiction and nonfiction, and the various cultural imports listed by Rice's lawyer, there were of course the American writers who were so widely read during the brilliant years, "l'entre-deux-guerres": Faulkner, Hemingway, Steinbeck, and Caldwell. With Dos Passos they made "les cinq grands," and they comprised, as Sartre says, along with jazz and "the large frescoes of [filmmaker King] Vidor, . . . the face of the United States" for thousands of young Frenchmen—a face "tragic, cruel, and sublime." [49]

In movies and television series dealing with the American West, the Chateaubriand-Cooper tradition has enjoyed fresh vigor. Most European (and some Asian) countries have tried their hand at producing Westerns and all have been susceptible to the influence of American movies. The gangster melodramas of Cagney and Bogart have also had an impact on foreign filmmakers who educated an ever-widening audience to familiarity with Europe's mythic America. The story of this impact occupies a large portion of most film histories, but other factors preparing the way for it are rarely discussed. I referred earlier to the cultural currents which have turned modern Russians and Germans toward the United States, and Golino has noted the encouragement provided by Italian fascist censorship. For France (as for England) the important impulse toward increased awareness of America came from the First World War. Prior to this there had been two French "discoveries" of America. The first had followed the visits of Lafayette and French participation in the Revolution. The second developed through French interest in the Civil War, and it persisted in a heartfelt enthusiasm for the prosperity of the gilded years—and a complementary desire to make the superiority of French culture balance its weaker economy. French novels of the era frequently picture an American businessman—often a widower—traveling with his daughter. There are a few lawyers, professors, doctors, even clergymen, but they all appear in the guise of the earlier hero, Benjamin Franklin.

They are businessmen, Simon Jeune remarks, "the only type which truly interests the French." Generous and fond of work, the American talks incessantly of money, be he "millionaire of 1860 or multimillionaire of 1900." [50] He is clearly—and quite unlike the earlier French notion of Franklin—a cultural barbarian.

"Up to 1914," notes André Bellessort, "America had provided for us romantic subjects of a diverse or curious type, and above all had given us the example of a great republic, of a great and prospering democracy which knew how to maintain the principle of authority almost intact and where things seemed generally to go much better than in our country." But, he continues, "the entrance into the war of the Americans and their arrival in France opened a new chapter in the history of our relations." [51] When American troops landed in France, the crass material might of the United States assumed the beneficent glow of certain victory for the Allies. Spiritual and cultural condescension gave way to a seemingly inexhaustible curiosity about the Americans and their country. America was no longer for Europeans another distant and exotic country among many; it had become demonstrably *the* nation of the present and the future.

I have made only incidental use of British writers and writing in this study both because the America of Dickens, Thackeray, Martineau, et al. has been frequently discussed, and because I think direct contact and common language diluted the imaginative invention which fed the richness of the American metaphor in Europe. But I would like to conclude this series of illustrations with one of the most persistent of modern myth-makers, D. H. Lawrence. The fourth chapter of this book concludes with Yves Berger's *The Garden,* a novel making self-conscious use of Europe's American metaphor. Lawrence, too, chose America as the traditional home of utopian experiment and source of Europe's religious, political, and cultural regeneration. In October 1915, when his hopes for a community on the Florida farm of Frederick Delius seemed near realization, Lawrence wrote Harriet Monroe:

Probably I am coming to America. Probably in a month's time, I shall be in New York. . . . I must see America: here the autumn of all life has set in, the fall: we are hardly more than

the ghosts in the haze, we who stand apart from the flux of
death. I must see America. I think one can feel hope there. I
think that there the life comes up from the roots, crude but
vital. Here the whole tree of life is dying. It is like being dead:
the underworld. I must see America. I believe it is beginning,
not ending.

"I believe America is my virgin soil: truly," he wrote Catherine
Carswell (December 1916), and added to Waldo Frank (July
1917):

> I believe America is the new World. Europe is a lost name,
> like Nineveh or Palenque. There is no more Europe, only a
> mass of ruins from the past.
>   I shall come to America. I don't believe in Uncle Samdom,
> of course. But if the rainbow hangs in the heavens, it hangs
> over the western continent. I very very very much want to
> leave Europe, oh, to leave England for ever, and come over to
> America.

Lawrence nursed his rejection of the Old World for seven years
before undertaking his pilgrimage in 1922. His journey to America, James C. Cowan has remarked, was "essentially a quest for
the symbols and myths whereby what he regarded as the waste
land of modern western civilization might be revived." [52] He
settled, not in Florida, but in New Mexico; in June 1924 he wrote
the Baroness von Richthofen: "Life in America is empty and
stupid, more empty and stupid than with us. I mean the city and
village life. But here, where one is alone with trees and mountains
and chipmunks and desert, one gets something out of the air,
something wild and untamed, cruel and proud, beautiful and
sometimes evil—that is really America. But not the America of the
whites." After a stay of three years, Lawrence returned to Europe,
a victim of the tuberculosis which would bring him the death he
now associated with "going west": "I don't feel like going back to
America," he wrote in February 1926. "I love the ranch, but I feel
a revulsion from America, from going west."

The quest from the first had been religious, and in religious
terms it was successful. "Behind the many gods of individual

places," Cowan observes, Lawrence saw "the unknown god of the unuttered name. Lawrence's religion is the worship of this unknown god. His American journey, on the mythic level, becomes a pilgrimage to the Sacred Mountain, the World Navel, in quest of the religious experience whereby the waters of the abyss might be loosed from this divine center to regenerate the waste land of modern civilization by engendering the creative impulse in both individual and society."

It was this impulse Lawrence got "out of the air" in the desert; its traces are clear in his *Studies in Classic American Literature* (1923), one of the greatest mythic readings of America (and perhaps the last).[53] For Lawrence America fulfilled some of its promise; for many another pilgrim it did not. But the certainty that a promise had been made is perhaps the supreme witness to the strength of Europe's American myth. It is only partly true to regard the steady stream of scientific and fictional discussion of America as creating that myth. The writings of Chateaubriand and Sealsfield affected the course of thousands of lives, but this was possible only because Europe wanted to believe. The dream of Paradise and Utopia helped inspire their books and the countless others which fed the myth and developed its characteristic imagery. And it determined in advance that Europe's America would be able to absorb all the negative connotations history and disappointed travelers might force upon it.[54]

III

The Invention of America: II

All the world was America.
—Locke

He has bound up in one abstract idea the whole of the
tendencies of modern commercial society.·. . .
—J. S. Mill

America is the new World. . . .
    There is no more Europe.
—D. H. Lawrence

Europe wanted to believe and still does. Even before the beginning of the modern period, "The American dream had
become part of the cultural tradition of Europe."[1] But such a
dream flourished best on half-truths at long distance. Villiers de
l'Isle-Adam's *The Eve of the Future* (1886) was accurate in its prediction that a new era was dawning with a future dominated by
America; our survey has taken us from the Europeanization of
America to the apparent Americanization of the entire world.
A major feature of Europe's American mirage has been wonder[2] —the wonder of fresh possibility for Europe, the wonder
Fitzgerald speaks of in *The Great Gatsby*. Once that wonder melts
in the heat of technological homogenization and earth-shrinking
communications, the European must choose one of two alterna-
tives. He may abandon the dream as chimerical, or—and this has
been the choice of most modern Europeans so far—he may

39

reaffirm its claim upon his imagination by the intensity with which he condemns those who have had the keeping of the dream but have failed in their charge. The villain here is Americanism, condemned by Augustin Léger in 1902 as "the force that will dominate our course, the invader that will transform our culture and our institutions, and will destroy the balance of the civilized world." [3] The virulence of the modern attacks on the quality of American life—attacks from within as well as without the United States—testifies poignantly to the need we all feel to believe in a more perfect world.

John Stuart Mill saw the implications of separating America from the normal course of human affairs many years ago; the temptation had proven irresistible to the redoubtable Tocqueville. "M. de Tocqueville," Mill complains, "has, at least apparently, confounded the effects of Democracy with the effects of Civilization. He has bound up in one abstract idea the whole of the tendencies of modern commercial society . . . thereby letting it be supposed that he ascribes to equality of conditions several of the effects naturally arising from the mere progress of national prosperity. . . ." [4] Or, as Henry Adams might have said, America's velocity of change has from the first simply been greater than Europe's. Philip Rahv has observed that

> what we think of as the modern era is perhaps simply the final synchronization of several different cultures into a single historical development. What American life and letters have always been elaborating, in a setting of social tensions and many kinds of violence, has also been working out in the past forty years in Europe and Soviet Russia—and now in lands and peoples remote from both. We are all now in social flux. We are all now face to face with vast natural and human forces and with many forms of violence springing from many forms of tension. What was once the epic age of an American microcosm has become an age of cosmic epic. It is exciting. It makes us live dangerously. But it is not kind and comfortable. Ages of great achievement seldom, if ever, are. The advantage for Americans—whether as artists or as

"ordinary men"—is that they have always lived in such an age, even if few of them were aware of it. The advantage for the rest of us is that we can learn much, for both our life and our letters, from their laboratory.[5]

In *Mr. Sammler's Planet* Saul Bellow's wonderful Punjabi, Dr. Govinda Lal, provides examples for both points I wish to make. The connotations of America will persist: Lal "seemed aware . . . that the discovery of America had raised hopes in the sinful Old World of a New Eden. 'A shared consciousness,' Lal had written [in his manuscript, The Future of the Moon], 'may well be the new America. Access to central data mechanisms may foster a new Adam.' " But, Lal remarks later, "Of course in a sense the whole world is now the United States. Inescapable . . . . It's like a big crow that has snatched our future from the nest, and we, the rest, are like little finches in pursuit trying to peck it." The obvious persistence and success of the finches leads me to think that in the future America will represent quite literally what Europe actually wants and will eventually get. If, as O'Gorman says, America has taken its meaning from the needs of Europe to extend and redefine itself, there are many indications that those needs have been filled, that *that* "America" is now complete and therefore no longer acquiring new meaning. One must always resist the temptation to see oneself at the juncture of historical movements, but it does seem that the last few years have been returning us to the unified world of the Renaissance. The more recent of the works examined in Part Two of this book treat America consciously as part of European folklore. And they do not confine their use of it to the representation of Europe's future: the United States has come to seem merely another manifestation of Europe's present, a common synonym for "modern." In 1958 Cyrille Arnavon asked whether the United States would be the country which, "as Mayakovsky said, monopolizes the name of its continent before perhaps coming to identify itself with the whole planet."[6] The answer would seem to be yes. This does not announce the end of the American metaphor. It points, rather, to a slowing, perhaps to a stoppage, of its rate of growth, its development, its accretion of connotations. All I mean to suggest is that this metaphor has now apparently stabilized and joined other poetic images—such as Fortune's wheel, or the world as stage—in a fixity of reference. When it is used henceforth it will call up specific historical associations; it cannot grow independently because America is no longer unique. America has become—as Professor McLuhan says—a world environment.

In "Americana" Giame Pintor admits that his remarks may not be historically accurate, may in fact have little to do with the actual United States. "But this does not matter because even if the continent did not exist our words would not lose their significance. This America has no need of Columbus, it is discovered within ourselves; it is the land to which we turn with the same hope and faith of the first immigrants . . . ." The history of *this* America not only predates the settlement and consequent founding of the United States; it doubtless also may have a lengthier future. Who knows, Leslie Fiedler's vision may well prove accurate: "One can foresee the discussion of five thousand years from now, when the scraps of . . . documents are being dug out of Italian soil, as to whether there ever was *really* an America, or only a metaphor like Atlantis, a fable for poets. . . ." [7]

PART TWO

America as Metaphor in Modern
European Literature

IV

A Fable for Poets

In European eyes, Americans have always appeared as
a kind of caricature, which I'm afraid is reflected in our
magazines and periodicals. We tend to think of you as a
race of cowboys wearing striped shirts and vulgar
loud shoes, which are absolutely necessary that you put
up on the table, while aggressively chewing your gum,
and wearing your hair down over your eyebrows because you simply don't have a forehead.
—Andrei Voznesensky, "Interview"

The European imagination, from Chateaubriand to
Kafka, has looked toward the western horizon whenever it turned from the citadels of constraint and
artifice back to Nature or forward to Utopia.
—TLS, "Castles and Culture"

In Part One I sought to detail the source and nature of the
American imagery inherited by modern European writers. My
principal interest in the pages which follow, however, is in the
uses these writers have found for these images and their accumu-
lated connotations. And that interest has naturally been strongest
where the artist and his work have approached the highest level of
achievement, where my subject is Kafka, Brecht, or Julian Green.
But before turning to a close examination of these authors, I want
to prepare as broad a context as I can. This essay is essentially an
introduction to the one which follows. As I move from examples

45

of simple stereotyping toward fully imagined and integrated metaphor, I try to survey briefly the aesthetic uses which a wide range of European writers have made of their legacy. Few of the examples I discuss are well known (although, almost without exception, they repay serious consideration). And criticism of them in English is often sparse or unsatisfying. Hence some interpretive summary has seemed unavoidable. I have kept my résumé to a minimum, however, hoping that my reader will turn to the full text if he wishes to appreciate the role played in the whole by the part under discussion.

Perhaps I should repeat a point stressed initially: my topic is not writing which concerns itself directly with America as subject or which turns primarily on its readers' curiosity about or interest in this country. These works I have been designating "local color" to distinguish them from artifacts which may be said to have claim to a greater degree of aesthetic autonomy. I do not for a moment, I should add, think that art can be free of political or social implication. But there is a discernible difference between writing which begins with ideas and proceeds to realize them artistically—the novel, play, or poem as essay—and literature which affects men's lives through aesthetic power. "The modern reader may be unaware of this," Eugène Vinaver has remarked in a similar context: "he may imagine that the survival of literature is determined by the importance of its message, the intrinsic interest of the matter, and its relation to human experience. His inability to seize upon the real sources of aesthetic enjoyment is no more surprising than any similar discrepancy between the real and the conventional criteria of value." [1] The present study focuses on this kind of power and the part various images of America have played in its achievement. At its base is the assumption that art differs fundamentally from expository argument, that the same materials used for different purposes will be used differently.

As I remarked earlier, the attitudes toward America produced by exploration, colonization, and immigration have demonstrated remarkable durability in the twentieth century. And once the impersonality of American technocracy is identified with the course of civilization itself, all the major elements of Europe's America are discernible. For the European writer, these elements have proven a popular source of ready-made stereotypes. Part One identifies three aspects of Europe's idea of America: the land of wilderness and the Noble Savage, a state of unlimited freedom and opportunity, and the technocratic civilization destined to dominate the world. I yielded to these simplifications there for the sake of convenience, and I will continue them here for the same reason, stretching them where I can and altering or abandoning them when I must. The literary materials of this study defy easy categorization; if they did not they would doubtless not sustain serious examination.

Except for the popularizations of the movies and writers like Karl May, the primitive America of Chateaubriand and Cooper has rarely attracted the modern European author. Perhaps it had become too familiar during the nineteenth century, or perhaps its very fancifulness made it resist serious use. As early as 1887 Chekhov can associate this fantastic America with the protagonists of his delightful story "Boys" who plan to run away across the Bering Straits to California—where "they don't drink tea but gin." The boys intend to dig for gold, to find ivory, fight tigers and savages and become pirates, for in America "one can get a living by hunting and plunder." [2] Thus for Chekhov one of Europe's fondest and most persistent illusions has come to seem no more than the daydream of schoolboys, a benchmark in a tale contrasting childhood and maturity. (Chekhov's intention appears similar in *Ivanov*, 1887. Near the end of Act II when Ivanov complains of his despair and self-contempt, Sasha jokingly suggests that they run away and begin life anew in America. A few moments later she declares her love and offers to go anywhere with him, even to the end of the world.)
Two elements of the boys' dream have proven durable for twentieth-century writers, however: the association of America with violence—an idea closely related to the impersonality of the modern city—and with escape. I will turn to the former in a few moments. I want first to examine some uses of America as else-

where, as not-Europe, as—frequently—the promised land, for it is in this capacity that it has served most often in European writing from the midnineteenth century onward.

The magical appeal of America as a world-more-attractive is elaborately rehearsed in Friedrich Gerstäcker's enormously popular *To America!* (1855):

"To America!"—Reader, can you still recall the tales in "A Thousand and One Nights," in which the tiny word "sesame" opens the gates to untold treasures for him who knows it? Have you heard of the magical incantations which in ancient times old wise men knew in order to call up ghosts from their graves and to employ the secret forces of the cosmos?—At the first sound of the simple syllable, as the saga has been handed down for centuries in the tradition of the people, lightning and thunder struck, the earth trembled, and the bold foolhardy soul who spoke the word reeled back before the dreadful force which it had conjured up.

Those times have passed; the spirits which then obeyed the race of man do so no more, or perhaps we may have forgotten the proper word to summon them—but have found instead another, which, hardly less potent, at one stroke tears the child from his parents' arms, the husband from his wife, the heart from all its relationships and ties, yes, from the earth of its homeland to which it until then had loyally clung with all its strongest and most intimate fibers.

"To America!" Lightly and boldly does the hothead audaciously call this out in the first and difficult hour which ought to test his strength, harden his mettle.—"To America!" whispers the desperate man who, on the verge of ruin, was here being pushed slowly but surely toward the abyss. —"To America!" says the destitute man quietly and resolutely; he, who has fought again and again with manly power against the force of circumstances, but always in vain, and who has prayed for his "daily bread" with bloody sweat—and yet has not received it, who sees no aid for himself or his loved ones here in the homeland, and yet will not beg, cannot steal. —"To America!" laughs the criminal after a successfully

executed robbery, exulting jubilantly in sight of the distant
shore which will provide him security from the arm of the
thus injured law.—"To America!" rejoices the idealist, who is
angry with the real world because it is in fact real, and who
envisages there, across the ocean, a prospect which conforms
more closely to the one conjured up in his own mad mind.
—"To America!" and with that single cry there lies closed off
behind them their entire former life, creation, labor—lie the
bonds which blood or friendship have here tied, lie the hopes
which they have nurtured here, the sorrows which oppressed
them—"To America!" [3]

Balzac's Vautrin embraces the dream in its more aristocratic
form. His plan is "to go and live the patriarchal life on a great
estate, say a hundred thousand acres, in the United States of
America, in the deep South. I intend to be a planter, to have
slaves, earn a few nice little millions selling my cattle, my tobacco,
my timber, living like a monarch, doing as I like. . . ." [4] But there
has been a tension between the dream of America and actual
arrival in the United States, a tension which has often led—in fact
and in fiction—to a return to the homeland. As a consequence, the
tale of temporary or permanent immigration has provided opportunity for a wide variety of statement about the power of the
human personality to discover, explore, expand—or lose— itself.
To cite an extreme example, Svidrigailov can echo Gerstäcker's
hypnotic "to America" when asked his destination, but he is
actually planning suicide. For Dostoevsky, as for Lermontov
before him, escape to America can become an ironic analogue for
total extinction. (Consider Pechorin in *A Hero of Our Time,* 1840:
"My soul has been warped by the world, my mind is restless, my
heart insatiable; nothing suffices me . . . . Only one expedient is
left for me, and that is to travel. As soon as possible I shall set
out—not for Europe, God forbid—but for America, Arabia, India—and perhaps I shall die somewhere on the road!" [5]) For
writers like Giraudoux or Sartre, however, America is simply
not-Europe, the place where Jerome Bardini can escape time and
space—"Truly it is only in America that one can walk incognito
among men" [6]—and Sortre's Gomez (in *Troubled Sleep,* 1949) can

be encapsulated in a life-as-usual New York to emphasize his recollection of wartime horror and his grief for the fall of France. Often the distance and differentness of America provide an author with the occasion for his character's renewal and return to new beginning in the homeland: "As soon as I arrive there with Grushenka," Mitya tells Alyosha in *The Brothers Karamazov* (1879-80),

> we shall set to work, working on the land, in a far-away place, in solitude, with the wild bears. I expect there, too, we shall be able to find a place away from people. There are still Red Indians there, I'm told, somewhere on the edge of the horizon. Well, it's there we shall go, to the last of the Mohicans. And, well, we shall at once apply ourselves to the study of grammar. . . . And in these three years we shall learn to speak English like any Englishman. And as soon as we've learnt it—goodbye to America! We'll run back here, to Russia, as American citizens.[7]

Gerhart Hauptmann's *Atlantis* (1912) provides a more complex and fully detailed example of this use of America. Hauptmann seems to have associated America largely with flight, the unsuccessful attempt to escape one's troubles and oneself. In *Dorothea Angermann* (1926), the heroine comes to America with hope for a new life; she finds instead a steady descent into immorality and crime. In the closely autobiographical treatment of his marriage problems, *Book of Passion* (1930), Hauptmann indicates that the American experience, and particularly his hero's admiration for Washington, D.C., is merely an impossible flight from self. America clearly holds no solutions. It may even, as in the dreams of Till Eulenspiegel, provide a setting for the most appalling injustice.

Hauptmann's earliest attempt to use the materials of his 1894 trip to America appeared as *Atlantis* in 1912. It is essentially a parable of rebirth, the story of Dr. Frederick von Kammacher's effort to build a new life outside Europe—a Europe where his stature as a scientist has been seriously discredited and his wife is incurably insane. His future is worked out in terms of two major emblems: the sea voyage on the *Roland* which occupies more than half the book, and the irrational passion for the young dancer Ingigerd which precipitates his emigration and ultimately provides the deepest sounding of his personality. Before he embarks, Frederick muses on this turning point in his life. He is moving, he decides, "away from Europe and his home. He seemed to be parting with a whole continent in his soul, upon which he would never set foot again. It was farewell forever." [8] But Frederick is given to categoric conclusions; this is but an instance of his faulty judgment, for the *Roland* proves to be an extension of Europe, a veritable microcosm of its culture. And the very difficulty of the voyage—the oppressive sense of discomfort and rolling sea is a major success of the novel—suggests what a struggle Frederick will undergo merely to test his separation from his native culture. Hauptmann sets his story in 1892 so as to recur again and again to the Columbus centennial, but Frederick's parallel to Columbus is colored by persistent irony: when he climbs to the ship's bridge to breast the sharp wind and revel in his growing sense of freedom and fresh beginning, he soon earns the laughter of the passengers when a wave breaks across the ship and drenches him to the skin. He eventually admits that he will have to fight for his new world. "My whole personality is being shaken through and through." [9]

There are even moments when Frederick becomes reconciled to the opulent old Europe of the *Roland.* "In the festive gleam of the countless electric lights, excited by the wine, the music and the rhythmic pulse-beat of the moving vessel, it seemed to him at times as if humanity in a festal procession with music playing were sailing to the Isles of the Blessed." [10] The ship at these moments bears a striking resemblance to the liner of Bunin's "The Gentleman from San Francisco." What Hauptmann thought of Frederick's vision can be seen in the sequel: the ship sinks with few survivors, and the America awaiting Frederick proves to be yet another Inferno. Chapter 33, "The Momentous Atlantis Dream," occurs very near the physical center of the book. Frederick realizes that a ship, any ship, is "an all-embracing symbol" which comprehends "all the wandering and adventuring of the human soul." [11] Ships recur throughout, and Europe and America seem the obvious extremities of man's journey—at least until Frederick surrenders his new-life fantasy and returns to Germany. The ship image, as embodied in the *Roland,* further suggests the need for immolation. Frederick dreams of sunken ships, and when the *Roland* goes down he is finally thrust, midway through the novel, into the new world he thinks he wants. Curiously (and not too convincingly) his wedding ring disappears with the ship. He will learn much later, when the plot requires it, that his wife is dead, but the symbolic liberation is complete when the *Roland* sinks.

In New York Frederick falls in at once with a former student and his lively group of emigrant German artists. He feels his new life has begun and sits down to breakfast "a 'new-born' man." But here again he is deceived. By saving Ingigerd from shipwreck he has carried his basic weakness from his old life to his new. The capricious, self-centered girl had initially entranced him with her dancing; in Europe her art seemed mysterious and hypnotic and became for Frederick an emblem for all his youthful, most romantic dreams. America offers him physical possession of Ingigerd, but the very harshness of taste and spotlight of notoriety which assure her theatrical success reveal to the maturing Frederick the vacuity and vulgarity of the girl's soul. America helps him free himself as he had been unable to do in Europe. The way is open for the final series of symbolic deaths and resurrections, the happy ending Hauptmann associates with return to Europe once the New World has performed its renovation.

At one point Frederick compares his infatuation with Ingigerd to the madness which drew the early explorers over the sea. In a not otherwise notably subtle book, the association of Ingigerd with both Frederick's youthful fantasies and his dream of a beautiful life in America makes a suggestive parallel to Europe's sense of the New World. She is youth and seductive mystery; in what is obviously a self-induced obsession, Frederick allows her to draw him from home, out to sea, through danger and discomfort toward a way of life totally alien to him; (the situation resembles that of Nabokov's *Lolita*). Frederick's father has approved the trip to America. Men whose lives are wrecked, he writes his son, often return as millionaires. But America's streets are not paved with gold, and the luxurious strands of Ingigerd's yellow hair frame a head which is—as Frederick is reminded—as empty as a doll's. Both Ingigerd and America help Hauptmann say that once an emigrant outgrows childhood illusion and confronts things as they are he will find that the values of his maturity draw him back to his European homeland.

The purpose Hauptmann would have the stay in America serve is nicely recapitulated when Frederick acquires a sailor's damaged clock. He will take it apart, he decides, and put it together so it will work properly. Then he will return it "to its home in Europe, Schleswig-Holstein, for which it was pining." [12] It is springtime in America as Frederick plans his trip to Europe; he is, in every important respect, already there. "I am, and will remain," he announces, "a European." [13] Hauptmann's *Atlantis* might be called an anti-immigration novel. It is a clear response to the flood of emigration guides and narratives that had begun in the previous century and showed no sign of abatement. In what must be a triumph of the genre which developed in opposition to the immigrant tale, Hauptmann's Frederick persuades all his close friends to join him in his return to Germany. (One might compare the more recent *Job,* 1930, by Joseph Roth. Its hero, Mendel Singer, decides that in America he has found no new world but the same old Europe—with more Jews in New York than in Kluczýsk. His story remains throughout essentially that of Job: the migration serves to challenge God, and the American locale allows separations, sudden successes and equally sudden reversals, the arbitrary disappearance and reappearance of family and friends. Roth's interest is centered in Mendel, and Mendel is always the Russian Jew, bewildered and isolated, thrown inward on his duel with God, never aware of the American environment except as it forces itself upon him to work the divine will. When the time of testing has passed, Mendel happily plans his return to Europe.[14])

The use of an extended—but limited—stay in America to affirm the superiority of Europe has been common, so common in fact that Cesare Pavese can assume it and ring some ironic changes in *The Moon and the Bonfire* (1950). Felix Moeschilin's *America-John's* (1933) draws on the same familiar pattern to give a comic twist to the formula. When Moeschilin's traveler returns to his village and tries to introduce his American values and American ways, the results are disastrous. Everything he does to help the formerly self-sufficient peasants harms them, for they cannot deal with the money he generously spreads among them. The last straw seems to be the presents he brings his mistress; once the previously compliant girls learn to expect rewards for their favors, the happy equilibrium of the village is destroyed. In Moeschilin's story Europe's ways appear the best after all.

I will turn in a moment to the immigrant tale itself, to the opportunities permanent dislocation have provided the writer who has chosen to utilize it. But there is another kind of visit to America which has provided a center for some remarkable writing. Bearing perhaps some relation to Europe's earliest primitivist fantasies, it brings its visitor directly to Goethe's basalt, to the bedrock foundation of primeval being. I have referred to Hauptmann's *Atlantis* because its use of America is both simple and typical of many European narratives. But where Frederick suffers illness and discomfort before arriving rather easily at his affirmation of European civilization, Jacob Wassermann's character, Warschauer-Waremme, is harrowed to the fiber of his cultural being as he learns the insufficiency of his Germanness for life in a modern world. The occasion for his test is his visit to the United States—through it the use of America to signify a trans-European, global culture enters the present discussion for the first time, and for the first time we see European civilization judged inadequate to the challenges of the modern world.

Wassermann's wife recalled that he wrote the first fifty pages of *The Maurizius Case* (1928) twenty-two times. His care is evident as the slowly deepening spiral of psychological analysis supplies persuasive evidence for the frequent comparison of Wassermann and Dostoevsky. The writing of the book was interrupted only once: when Wassermann spent almost three months in America during 1927. Some of his observations are transferred to the novel, but every American detail is made to contribute something to the book's larger concerns: a tale of guilt, justice, and individual responsibility, with the seemingly marginal use of America actually playing a very important role in the definition of the novel's most enigmatic character.

Wassermann's books return frequently to a single theme: the

bewildering complexity, the impenetrable layers of human personality. In *The Maurizius Case,* he creates a rich psychological challenge in the man of two names, Warschauer-Waremme, the perjured key witness in the Maurizius case. In a series of encounters set many years after the trial, the sixteen-year-old Etzel—playing detective and trying to reopen the case—finally gets Warschauer to reveal his past. Warschauer is a man of capacious mind and tremendous experience. The efforts of Etzel to trick him into talking are transparent to him: he tells Etzel to stop playing the Indian. But though only in his forties, he now feels old and alone, and so he eventually begins his story.

Born the Jew Warschauer, he did everything he could to escape his Jewish heritage. He not only hated the Jewish people and the whole Jewish outlook, but he also saw his past as a hindrance to the public success he hoped to achieve. Wassermann is careful to impress us with Warschauer's intellectual power. We are ready to believe that he was in fact suited for the brilliant career he sought. He decided to become a German, and for a while he was successful. He changed his name to Waremme, was baptized a Christian, and enjoyed total acceptance and growing fame. "Invisible hands had paved my way. The years at the university, Breslau, Jena, Frieburg—always going from east to west—a series of triumphal stations. Yes, from east to west, always farther, from the depths to the heights, then to the depths again, to the very depths: from east to west like the sun." [15] Unlike Perse's use of movement toward the west, Wassermann's plan for Warschauer's life is cyclic. Warschauer fails to protect himself against setback, and when all comes to nothing he can only continue toward the west—a pattern which he himself uses to order his life for Etzel and to imply both hope and an inevitable decline and destruction. At first he planned to leave Europe and recoup his losses across the Atlantic. But he soon came to accept his life as a total failure; there would never be a triumphant German homecoming. He faced the choice of Svidrigailov: "I finally knew that there was no return. There was for me either a bullet through my head, or . . . burning my ships behind me, not looking back, losing myself, an unknown person in an unknown world. This is what happened." [16]

Thus the third phase of life begins for Warschauer-Waremme,

the "overseas-international." In terms of the novel's plot, his decade in America is simply a convenient device for removing him from the Europe of Maurizius and his case. But Wassermann also pursues the psychological effects of Warschauer's migration and their implication for any ultimate assessment of European culture—an assessment worked out with America as foil but clearly intended as defense of the Jewish tradition Warschauer had rejected in his youth.

It is not easy for the self-made German national to cut those carefully cultivated roots. "To turn one's back upon Europe does not yet mean to be able to live without it." [17] And so he persuades himself that he emigrates largely "to proclaim the spirit of Europe." He will be "Columbus the Second. The apostle Paul of civilization and culture." [18] At this point Wassermann has achieved a fully convincing and dramatic confrontation: he is ready to use America to sound the depths of his highly intelligent, wholly self-conscious German Jew. "I had to calculate, to settle the accounts. . . . Warschauer *versus* Waremme, you understand. The one side and the other: two parties. Europe and the past; America and the future: more and more this became the leitmotif." [19] Warschauer's American years are a descent to the Inferno, a hell of poverty, loneliness, and racial violence. Not only does his European culture fail to sustain him but it comes to seem irrelevant. Like Kafka's Karl Rossmann and Pavese's Anguilla, this self-styled Columbus never finds his bearings:

> I stepped into the street for a moment, the confused tangle of people and motor-trucks, the whirling eddies of dust, the screaming colours of the advertisements, the lead-coloured sky, it was a moment when one no longer understands one's own existence. Perhaps you are on the moon, I thought, perhaps this is a city in the moon and these are its inhabitants, these ghosts and furies are living in deserts of craters and lava. [20]

Warschauer's American adventure gives Wassermann an opportunity to turn him inside out. It is significant that the lengthy stay in the United States is compressed into Warschauer's recollections before Etzel, some twenty pages in a novel of over five hundred. Wassermann is not interested in describing America but in using it as an expository foil to his extraordinary War-schauer. Warschauer himself uses his anecdotes to impress Etzel with the profound depths of human personality as yet beyond the reach of the boy's understanding.

Warschauer is deprived not only of himself—of the self he had so laboriously created—he also loses his faith in the universal viability of European culture. He comes to believe that the future he has beheld in America will pass Europe by; it will belong to the United States and to Russia, and to the inevitable confrontation between the two which lies ahead. The distance Warschauer has traveled in his apostleship of civilization and culture is empha-sized when he concludes that "In contrast to this glowing crater, Europe was a cabinet of antiquities." [21] When he accepts this he must give up his European self and reaffirm his Jewishness. America has thus served to strip Wassermann's character of his European veneer, and he must undertake the construction of his personality once more. (In Max Frisch's *I'm Not Stiller,* 1954, America provides both Stiller and Sibylle with an opportunity for self-definition. Yet another rejection of European culture occurs in Franz Werfel's fantasy of the future, *Star of the Unborn,* 1946. The protagonist thinks of the Jungle—Europe—as his home, but when he flees the efficiency of Panopolis—America—in an effort to reclaim his heritage, he discovers that the Jungle is for him no longer habitable. Unlike Warschauer, he rejects Europe and re-turns to make a life in futuristic America.)

In 1853 a group of Italian peasants sent the following note to the Bourbon minister of the interior:

> Your Excellency: His Majesty's faithful subjects beg to in-form Your Excellency that the woods belonging to both charitable institutions and private individuals are being cut down and the land cleared for cultivation, to the detriment of our pastures. For lack of firewood the undersigned and all other inhabitants of the Abruzzi region will be compelled to emigrate to California.[22]

Presumably some compromise was reached, for there is no evidence that everyone in the region moved to California. Thousands of Europeans, however, did flee their past and present to pursue their future in the United States, and the sheer weight of their migration spawned countless books aimed directly at potential immigrants or those curious about the experience of the migrants. There are descriptions of the voyage and the difficulties of adjustment, advice on farming techniques, and warnings against exploitation. The immigrant novel also permitted the introduction of American lore likely to satisfy a more general curiosity, an interest in the exotic idiosyncrasies of local color.

But there is a third aspect to the immigrant adventure, and it is only at this level that it has held the attention of the serious artist. The long extract from Gerstäcker's *To America!* quoted above suggests the variety of human passion, the possibility of isolation, of confrontation, of success and failure, that can be introduced easily into stories of immigration. I have not come upon a first-rate fiction which treats successful transplantation—unless Kafka's expressionistic fragment be viewed this way. Perhaps the unfamiliarity of actual American life renders such treatment difficult. Or perhaps, since by my definition the authors I cite are more interested in the coherence of their artifacts than in the details of upheaval, the move abroad remains always simply a useful expedient to be integrated into the larger rhythms of their narratives. Whatever the reason, the materials I have come to value remain essentially European; their uses of the move to America are reactive, ironic, and satiric.

A frequent lament of European cultural commentators during the first half of the century was that the United States had been swallowing Europe, that France, Germany and Italy had been Americanized, "cocacolonized" beyond recognition. Italy and America are culturally very different, Giuseppe Prezzolini complains, "and the only effect that recently improved communications have had, has been that America, the stronger and more vital of the two, has invaded Italy not only with its industrial products . . . but also with its literary fashions and with its way of life." [23] Writers like Alberto Moravia regularly invoke America as an emblem of efficiency, power, and success. In Silone's Pietro Spina novels, *Bread and Wine* (1937) and *The Seed Beneath the Snow* (1940), America is no golden mystery for the lucky immigrant to fathom; it is instead posited as a temptation to neglect the problems of the homeland. To a Marxist like Silone, if the Abruzzi peasants who threatened the minister had emigrated to California, they would have abandoned their land in a time of need and chased an empty vision across the sea. He rejected as well the imaginary escape to America to evade time and its responsibilities that plays such an important part in Carlo Levi's *Christ Stopped at Eboli.* Silone often selected the peasant who accepted such a dream—like Sciatap in *Bread and Wine*—as a betrayer of his nation's hope. The point is stressed in *Fontamara* (1930) where the vicious exploitation of the countryside by the Impresario is associated with the same evocative America:

> "The Impresario has discovered America right here, that's. the truth."
> "America?" the others answered. "America is far away and doesn't look like this."
> "America is everywhere," the Impresario told those who referred the argument to him. "It's everywhere, you just have to know how to look for it." [24]

Carlo Levi's superb narrative, *Christ Stopped at Eboli* (1945), can serve to illustrate both what one large peasant population believed about America (a population which contributed heavily to the stream of migration) and what an imaginative artist might do with this myth as myth.

"The history of a day," remarks Melville's narrator in describing the lives of the natives of Typee, "is the history of a life." Levi's book deals with similar lives. He creates a sense of suspended time through the isolation of his Calabrian peasants, the circularity of their daily routine, their superstition—and the stasis of a future embodied in mythic emigration to America. Apart from the narrator, the story has no center—only the peasants. The setting is a village in the south, but as the endpaper maps and the other towns described and visited make clear, the life remarked includes at least half the nation. And there is no reason to limit Levi's vision to Italy; it would seem to evoke what he calls the pre-Christian peasantry wherever it may yet endure. For the distinguishing characteristic of these lives is their immunity to time and history.

Levi's book turns smoothly on an opposition between two worlds—what he calls the post-Christian, modern civilization of Naples, Rome, and America, and the pre-Christian (hence his title), primeval death-in-life of the peasantry. Perhaps it is because the narrator is himself a northerner with an appetite for irony that his central symbol for the twentieth century provides one of the book's rare comic moments:

> In the middle of this square there was a strange monument, almost as high as the houses around it and endowed by the narrowness of the place with a certain solemnity. It was a public toilet, the most modern, sumptuous, and monumental toilet that can be imagined, built of concrete, with four compartments and weatherproof overhanging roof, of the type that has only recently been put up in the big cities. On one wall stood out in huge block letters an inscription of the makers' name, familiar to city-dwellers: "Renzi & Co., Turin." What strange circumstances, what magician or fairy had borne this marvelous object through the air from the faraway North and let it fall like a meteorite directly in the middle of this village square, in a land where for hundreds of miles around there was no water and no sanitary equipment of any kind? It was a by-product of the Fascist government and of the mayor, Magalone, and, judging by its size, it must have cost the yield of several years of local taxes. I looked inside: a pig was drinking the stagnant water at the bottom of one receptacle; two children were floating paper boats in another. In the course of the year I never saw it serve any other function. I saw no one enter it but pigs, dogs, chickens, and children except on the evening of a feast day in September, when a few peasants climbed up on the roof to get a better view of the fireworks. Only one person put it to the use for which it was intended, and that was myself. Even so I must confess that I did so less from necessity than on account of a certain homesickness.[25]

Immediately after making this remark, the narrator notices, "in one corner of the square, which barely escaped falling within the long shadow cast by the monument, a lame man, dressed in black with a wizened, solemn, almost priestly face, as thin as that of a polecat. . . ." The man is blowing into an incision made on the hindleg of a freshly killed goat—as an aid in removing its skin, so it turns out. But the goat lies on an altarlike platform, and to see the man with the almost priestly face "attached in this way to the animal, whose form was gradually inflated, while he seemed silently to grow thinner and thinner as he emptied himself of his breath recalled some strange sort of metamorphosis whereby a man is changed into a beast." [26] It is hardly possible to suggest how pervasive such imagery is in Levi's book. It goes beyond mere contrast with the toilet in the town square, and the suggestion throughout that peasants and animals are interchangeable eludes the simple conclusion that the fascist state has deprived its citizens of their humanity. The ambiguities of the imagery are repeatedly emphasized in the narrator's reactions. He not only notes the irrelevance of modern civilization to the world of the peasants, but he also senses the strength they have found in their absolute identification with all earthly things.

The same doubleness marks the narrator's reference to America. There is, of course, the fact of emigration and return: the village has twelve hundred inhabitants, many of whom once made what they thought was a permanent move to America only to be frightened back to Italy in 1929 or trapped one way or another during the customary nostalgic return to visit with old friends. And there are over two thousand men from the village who have left and who will never return. But with his curious mixture of distance and comprehension, the narrator uses the peasants' vision of America—which he knows to be a myth—as yet another image of life lived outside time and outside hope. As a doctor, the narrator visits nearly every house in the village during the course of the year. He is repeatedly struck by two

inseparable guardian angels that looked at me from the wall over the bed. On one side was the black, scowling face, with its large, inhuman eyes, of the Madonna of Viggiano; on the other a colored print of the sparkling eyes, behind gleaming glasses, and the hearty grin of President Roosevelt. I never saw other pictures or images than these: not the King nor the Duce, nor even Garibaldi; no famous Italian of any kind, nor any one of the appropriate saints; only Roosevelt and the Madonna of Viggiano never failed to be present. To see them there, one facing the other, in cheap prints, they seemed the two faces of the power that has divided the universe between them. But here the roles were, quite rightly, reversed. The Madonna appeared to be a fierce, pitiless, mysterious, ancient earth goddess, the Saturnian mistress of this world; the President a sort of all-powerful Zeus, the benevolent and smiling master of a higher sphere. Sometimes a third image formed, along with these two, a trinity: a dollar bill, the last of those brought back from across the sea, or one that had come in the letter of a husband or relative, was tacked up under the Madonna or the President, or else between them, like the Holy Ghost or an ambassador from heaven to the world of the dead.[27]

If men without a country can be said to have a capital city, the narrator notes, then for the peasants the capital is neither Rome nor Naples but New York. "And it *is* their capital, in the only way it can be for them, that is as a myth." [28] It is a paradise, "Jerusalem the golden," and it is as unattainable. Even the immigrant remains always on the outside and quite untouched by the actual America he encounters. The narrator is told about a group in New York which used to meet every Sunday for an outing in the country:

There were eight or ten of us: a doctor, a druggist, some tradesmen, a hotel waiter, and a few workers, all of us from the same town and acquainted with each other since we were children. Life is depressing there among the skyscrapers, where there's every possible convenience, elevators, revolving doors, subways, endless streets and buildings, but never a bit of green earth. Homesickness used to get the better of us.

On Sundays we took a train for miles and miles in search of some open country. When finally we reached a deserted spot, we were all as happy as if a great weight had been lifted from our shoulders. And beneath a tree, all of us together would let down our trousers. . . . What joy! We could feel the fresh air and all of nature around us. It wasn't like those American toilets, shiny and all alike. We felt like boys again, as if we were back in Grassano; we were happy, we laughed and we breathed for a moment the air of home. And when we had finished we shouted together: *"Viva l'Italia!"* The words came straight from our heart.[29]

Clearly the "shiny and all alike" advantages of America are as meaningful as the concrete monument in the village square. But the myth of America remains untouched; it is the same for those who return to the village and those who never leave.

By way of indicating what I take to be the central implication in Levi's use of the American myth, I want to digress briefly to discuss "The Boy," a short story by Giuseppe Antonio Borgese which turns on the same point. An inexperienced young man goes to Genoa on a business errand for his father. In a restaurant he becomes fascinated by two men and a woman, "people of another race, born beneath another sky. The two men were tall and blond. They laughed heartily and aloud, moving their arms in casual but sweeping gestures. They wore large pearls in the buttonholes of their white shirts. Between them sat a woman who was also tall and blond. Her throat and shoulders were bare, half veiled with misty silk, violet like haze on a distant mountain in the morning sunshine. Marvelous to his eyes, she bore the divinity of a princess. . . . Clearly wealthy, they were 'Americans,' 'millionaires,' strong and alive with the joy of existence." Borgese's boy has no need to dream, for his princess takes the initiative and spends the night in his room. When she ignores him the next day, he says, "Tomorrow." She stops to look in her dictionary and answers, "No tomorrow." [30]

The expectations and harsh reality of the brief exchange point nicely to the America of *Christ Stopped at Eboli.* In Borgese's story the boy refuses to separate dream and actuality: he insists the woman is his wife, then calls her a whore and shoots her. But the static timelessness of Levi's village is figured in the persistence with which it insulates its mythic America from such a confrontation: America remains eternal promise, the tomorrow that cannot exist in a world where past and present are identical. The word most often heard in the village is *crai,* "from the Latin *cras,* tomorrow. Everything that they are waiting for, that is due to come, that should be remedied or attended to is *'crai.'* " But as the narrator remarks, " *'crai'* means 'never.' " [31]

Ruggero, the village womanizer of Livia de Stefani's fine novel *The Passion of Rosa* (1958), actually secures the fresh start he seeks in America. He persuades his simple wife, Rosa, that his emigration is necessary to repair the family fortunes. Rosa, of course, understands the magic of America: "In America," she tells her father, "men much older than you are—seventy or even eighty— get married and have children and go swimming in the sea. . . ." "—In America," her mother sighs, as if she had said, "In Paradise." [32] Ruggero is "longing to show what I'm made of —that I'm the kind of man who'll jump at any job where there's quick money to be made and a bit of fun to be had." He has always felt that he looks like Gregory Peck, and he dreams of a film career, Cadillacs, and "a house in Bel Air, with a swimming pool in the garden." [33] Though he keeps it from Rosa, he also dreams of blonde American women who wear tiny bikinis and drive enormous cars. California: "That was where Hollywood was . . . and the gold mines, and he had heard that the earth was so full of oil that you only had to make a hole in it with a screwdriver and the stuff spurted out. And the girls were wonderful; you could see pictures of them in all the magazines. They all had cars of their own, and they looked gay and glamorous, and ready to fall into your arms the moment you whistled to them. That was the life for him." [34]

"My husband doesn't write from America / What can I have done to offend him," go the lyrics from an Italian song.[35] For a time Rosa's trust is proof against Ruggero's failure to write, but once she is persuaded to inquire after him at the U.S. embassy, she unwittingly accelerates the bureaucratic machinery which will crush both her husband and herself.

With nice irony, Ruggero finds his America, and it provides a broad stage and sufficient temptation to reveal his weak character. He falls in with racketeers, makes money, drives a big car, and ultimately marries a blonde American and settles in a bungalow near Santa Monica—with washing machine, refrigerator, and "central heating." Even after he is apprehended and imprisoned, he remains true to his dreams: once released he means to hunt uranium and make a quick fortune. But real America finds him undesirable and sends him home. Rosa is willing to forgive. She hopes to win back his love, and when she is advised to look more like American girls, she has her hair curled and her nails manicured. She applies lipstick and perfume, shaves under her arms, and—after some agonized deliberation—pads her brassiere. She even agrees not to press charges for bigamy, but Ruggero is not wise enough to keep hidden the contempt he has always felt for her. As the novel nears its catastrophic close, Rosa realizes at last what her position has been. The emotional upheaval aggravates anew the bullet Ruggero earlier planted in her breast, and she races feverishly through the unfamiliar city in a deliberate—and successful—effort to bring on her death, a death which will destroy Ruggero as well. She has been naïve and sentimental throughout, and her death might well seem the fruit of an excessively passionate nature. But the careful symbolism of this well-constructed novel suggests that there is more to this final scene than that. Many Italian stories pit the man of the soil against the crushing forces of urban, industrial life, and it seems fair to see an embodiment of the conflict in this final tableau. Rosa's elementary innocence has only a light peasant shawl for protection against the chill night, the dark city street, and the burning wound near her heart. The wound recalls the evil of Ruggero, a peasant emptied by illusion, and it is mortal. Clearly a metaphor for the inhuman sterility of modern life, America provides de Stefani with all the detail she needs to build a rich and powerful novel.

Much modern European literature has turned on gullibility and hasty embrace of illusion—perhaps for obvious political reasons. For many writers mentioned in the present study, America has proven a viable metaphor for that credulity, a faith undoubtedly justified in seeking the future across the Atlantic but usually unprepared for what actually lies ahead. De Stefani's *Rosa* has brought us once again to Europe's association of America with the world of tomorrow, but before turning to the vast literature which has drawn on these connotations, I want to mention two humorous efforts to deflate the illusions mentioned above. With whimsical, affectionate condescension, Vladimir Korolenko uses the early pages of *In a Strange Land* (1895) to prick the pride of his villagers, their credulity, and their ignorance of the outside world. The peasants live in "a quiet, silent, slumbering country," [36] and America is used to evoke the wonders of experience outside the village orbit. When the husband's letter arrives to summon his wife to America, it is not actually delivered for a week while the villagers argue over its contents. The steamship ticket means wealth, freedom, "Liberty," but any effort to grasp the sums involved or make direct application of the abstractions only serves to reveal the limited provincialism of the villagers. Korolenko could have used any test of his peasants' ignorance to secure his gentle humor; he sought a concrete referent familiar enough to his audience to reveal the joke and yet sufficiently exotic to make the peasants' incomprehension believable, and he chose America and the complexities of immigration.

Giuseppe Berto's "Aunt Bess, In Memoriam" is far more bitter in its burlesque of misplaced faith. The story brings together a remarkable number of European assumptions and then turns them upon its Italian family in a caustic spoof of popular credulity. Anyone who has read the earlier pages of this book will recognize the imaginative clichés Berto draws upon; and although the narrator's father provides the tale with its focus—"a stupendous combination of Buffalo Bill and Henry Ford"—it is the narrator himself who shares in the myth-making which forms the central action of the story. When the children are tempted to doubt that their father had ever prospected in the Klondike, they have to admit

> several irrefutable facts. Apart from our names—Tom, Mike (yours truly), Johnny, and Peggy; apart from the existence of a photograph of a man, clumsy-looking as a bear, and perfectly capable of being our father, posed in front of a snow-

covered mountain; apart from the determination every
Sunday morning with which the man who had fathered us,
foregoing mass, set out to pan for gold along the banks of our
gentle plains river; apart from all this—there was Aunt Bess:
a remote and mysterious personage who once each year, at
Christmas, sent us a package of presents from an inconceiv-
able place called Wichita Falls, Texas, U.S.A.[37]

The precise relationship of Aunt Bess to the family has become
clear to the children only gradually. The silence of the grand-
parents on the subject, the glare the mother directs at the father
when Aunt Bess is mentioned—the children conclude with evident relish that

Aunt Bess was not an aunt at all. She was merely someone
with whom our father had taken up during this glorious
American adventure. . . . Aunt Bess, clearly, must have been
one of those marvelous western vamps—the kind that dances
and shows her thighs through a slit in her skirt, singing
huskily as she slinks from table to table plucking men's
billfolds, one of those that finally, when her lover-bandit
arrives, blows out all the lights in the saloon with her six
shooter.[38]

The children piece the story together: Bess had helped their
father when he failed in the Klondike, but instead of staying with
her he had returned to Italy. "If our father had preferred all this
to America, then he was nothing." They might have been the
children of Aunt Bess instead of their actual mother. "We had
gone so far as even to decide upon American professions for us.
Tom would have been a pimp, Johnny ringleader of a gang of
crooks, and I, the lazy idealist, a lighthouse keeper to whom
beautiful women would flee in hiding from the police." [39] In
rejecting both father and mother in favor of Bess, America, the
source of all gifts and all blessings, the children earn their come-
uppance. After the war when there is no food, they write Aunt
Bess for help. They receive a letter and a packet of powder, and
since they cannot read English they turn to brewing soup with the

powder; it is wrapped with a red, white, and blue ribbon and (like D'Annunzio) they decide a whole continent has come to their rescue. But it is not help but Aunt Bess herself who has arrived. All too late the letter is deciphered: "I regret to inform you that dear Bess has passed on. . . . She bequeathed herself to you. . . . With this parcel I am carrying out her will." [40]

Like Silone, Berto would attack any illusion which kept one from helping himself. The American myth serves him well because—like Korolenko before him—he can rely on its familiarity to his audience. There appears to be a single element which has ensured the longevity and omnipresence of Europe's American dream from its very inception. From first to last, America has signified money to the European. The quest for wealth dominated most journeys of exploration, and the "fresh start" motivating much immigration assumed the availability of at least economic sufficiency, and usually much more. This idea pervaded Europe before mass migration began; once it started, the undeniable fact that many did improve their condition here—and often wrote or returned home to demonstrate their luck—ensured a viable cluster of accepted associations for the writer electing to use the appropriate American counters. Every European knew that America meant wealth, that wealth meant business, that business meant capitalism and the capitalist, and that—basically—the source of all good things, at least in the twentieth century, was technology. These identifications have survived every pressure the modern era has brought to bear: the market crash, depression and unemployment, and—most potent in some countries—the criticism and challenge of communism and Soviet mythological competition. Most Europeans could scorn Silone's Impresario and the economic gangsters of Wedekind and Brecht, but no one could doubt that they represented a certain kind of success or that this success was properly thought of as "American."

Certainly the stereotypical capitalist did not need the celebrity of attack by the Soviets to ensure his survival (cf. "L'Oncle Sam" of nineteenth-century French drama), but it has undoubtedly helped. Maxim Gorky was a powerful and influential image-maker. When the cool reception he received in New York [41] reinforced his ideological need to attack America, he launched a series of sketches which sharpened the images of the capitalist and capitalist society throughout Europe. "The most remarkable thing," Leonid Andreyev recalled, "is that while in his stories and articles about America Gorky wrote nothing but the very worst that could be said about the country he never told me anything but the very best about America." [42] Gorky might write to Andreyev of "an amazing fantasy of stone, glass, and iron" and "stormy souls full of wild energy," [43] but his public utterance was devastating. His reception by the New York of 1906 must be held at least partly responsible for the bloated American capitalist who dominates much Soviet literature using American materials: "The City of the Yellow Devil" and "One of the Kings of the Republic" have supplied Soviet propagandists with an enduring American image. In the absence of free travel and cultural interchange during the Stalin period, Gorky's brutal businessman and nightmare New York served most Soviet writers as automatic counters when they wrote of America or sought to draw upon the associations it could be made to call up.

The purpose of this chapter is to illustrate the use and transcendence of stereotypes most of us know well. Although Gorky was a gifted and skillful writer, his America is simply a local-color ideological target. A brief glance at it will serve two purposes, however. It will summarize succinctly and colorfully the capitalist type used so fruitfully by later writers, and it will provide a rare opportunity to observe the deliberate enrichment of figurative connotation. Gorky knew what he was doing when he set out to develop his capitalist type, and the governmental officials who have regularly republished these pieces have understood exactly what he accomplished.

There is no quest for operative setting or character development in Gorky's sketches: the satiric picture of America is obviously an end in itself. Here is an exchange between the narrator-interviewer and a tycoon in his "One of the Kings of the Republic" (1906). The businessman is asked, "Do you consider yourself a Christian?"

"I certainly do!" he exclaimed. . . . "But . . . at the same time I am an American and, as such, a strict moralist. . . ."

... "What exactly do you mean?" I inquired lowering my voice.

"Let this be between us!" he warned me in a whisper. "It is impossible for an American to recognize Christ!"

"Impossible?" I whispered after a slight pause.

"Decidedly," he confirmed in a whisper.

"But why?" I queried after a moment's silence.

"He was born out of wedlock!" The old man winked at me.

... "Do you understand? A man born out of wedlock . . . is not received anywhere in decent society. . . . Oh, we are very strict! And if we were to recognize Christ, we would also have to accept all the illegitimately born as respectable people. . . . Think how horrible that would be! Eh?" [44]

This imaginary interview and the expressionistic sketch, "The City of the Yellow Devil" (1906?) are central documents for any study of Europe's image of America. It is not only that Gorky's pictures dominate later Soviet descriptions of America, both direct and metaphoric (e.g. Mayakovsky), but also that echoes of his nightmare city and brutal millionaire can be heard in the work of Kafka, Brecht, Céline, and many others. Gorky seems a camera floating through a hallucinatory New York, a city of gold where lust for the dollar destroys humanity and melts individuals into the mindless anonymity of mobs. From the opening page, where the arriving ship moves through muddy water, fog, and smoke, the details anticipate Kafka: "The massive figure of the bronze woman is covered from head to foot with verdigris. The cold face stares blindly through the fog, out to the wastes of ocean, as though the bronze is waiting for the sun to bring light to its lifeless eyes." [45] As in the work of Céline, this gaze never melts. There is nothing to illumine the sterile panorama of New York except the cruel glint of gold and the remarkable phantasmagoria of electric lights—the same lights which dominate the American metaphors of Mayakovsky. Gorky's millionaire capitalist served as prototype for dozens of villains in European literature, and I shall have occasion to mention him again in this book. For the moment it is enough to recall a single speech, for it sums Gorky's premises and

illustrates his tone and forthright approach. The interviewer has
secured the millionaire's opinion on religion, on the poor, on
government. He turns to art. "Music," he is told, "should be
patriotic. A march is always good, but American marches are the
best. America is the best country in the world; that is why
American music is the best on earth. Good music is always to be
found among good people. The Americans are the best people on
earth. They have the most money. No one has as much money as
we have." [46]

   To quote Gorky out of context like this is to highlight the
humorous possibilities his capitalist was bound to suggest to
writers less committed to propaganda. Gorky's friend Leonid
Andreyev [47] uses his simple capitalist in *Satan's Diary* (1920) as a
comic foil to emphasize the paradoxical unworldliness of a Satan
who has sought amusement by preempting the body and personality of an American millionaire. In Ilya Ehrenburg's *The
Extraordinary Adventures of Julio Jurenito and His Disciples* (1922),
Gorky's businessman is drawn further and further away from his
initial equation with American capitalism to become a complex
metaphor for the anarchic forces tearing the world apart. Once
underway, the novel gradually loses the lightness of its initial
picaresque buffoonery and acquires a bitterly Brechtian edge, but
roughly a third of the story is used to introduce the nihilistic
anarchist Jurenito and his disciples, and most of this turns on
what I have been calling local color. Ehrenburg makes easy game
of national foibles and familiar human absurdities. In this way
M. Delet and Mr. Cool can be viewed simply as a sensual French
rentier and Gorky's ludicrous capitalist, "faithful," as the narrator
records, "to the traditions of American multi-millionaires." [48]

   But despite its episodic structure, this novel has a coherent and
serious philosophic base; the symbolic freight carried by both
Delet and Cool quickly exceeds mere French and American idio-
syncrasy. When we first meet Mr. Cool he seems simply a fresh
copy of Gorky's omnipotent American financier, set down, for the
moment, in an office right out of Chaplin's *Modern Times* (the
narrator later praises Chaplin). "He tended to apply the methods
of a telephone conversation to ordinary intercourse. One night,
sitting alone in a restaurant and feeling bored, he suddenly

barked at a passing actress: 'Hello! Woman? Cool speaking. Are you free? Want to come with me? Hello! let me have an estimate. . . .' " [49] Touches like this promise to take Cool far beyond Gorky's cardboard figure and perhaps turn him into a comic creation of the first order, but once induced to supply financial support for Jurenito's schemes, Cool seems to slip from Ehrenburg's mind. Wildly comic invention is lavished instead on Delet, and it is his speech, his eating and lovemaking habits which bear the brunt of Ehrenburg's attack on self-seeking opportunism. But Delet and Cool are really the same figure; their identity is emphasized by their partnership at the book's close. These two alone survive the war unscathed and return to exploitation and profit-taking. At the level of ideas, Delet-Cool emerge as by far the most destructive force Jurenito has enlisted. Delet's sensualism, his elementary pleasure-pain philosophy, is associated by Ehrenburg with the Frenchman's preoccupation with death (he dreams of a "Universal Necropolis" with profits to feed his appetites). Cool's implications are at once more ambitious and complex, which may account for his lack of clear definition in the book. Gorky's financier had relied for strength on two books, the Bible and the Ledger. Cool also invokes the Bible and his checkbook, but once Ehrenburg has linked his millions to racketeering carried on in the name of religion, Cool is no longer a funny character nor does he seem simply American—as witness the later collaboration of M. Delet. The novel's close parallels Brecht's *St. Joan of the Stockyards;* it cannot be called comic, nor can it be localized in American business.

The most artistically successful use of Gorky's stereotype that I know was written by his countryman, Nobel laureate Ivan Bunin. Bunin resisted Soviet aesthetic dogma (he emigrated to France in 1919), so perhaps he felt the aims of propaganda insufficient. Whatever the reason, his justly famous "The Gentleman from San Francisco" (1915) introduces its American capitalist only to use him as the focal point of a tale whose complexity has rarely been acknowledged.

Few stories appear more simple and direct at first encounter. Although Bunin is more restrained and artful than Gorky, his

American millionaire never reaches beyond caricature, and
Bunin's condemnation of his wealth and his values is always
evident. After having dedicated himself to accumulating a fortune, the Gentleman turns to enjoying life. With his wife and
daughter he travels luxuriously until a stroke induced by overindulgence brings him death. The point might seem to lie in the
transformation this death works among those who had been
serving the Gentleman and his family so obsequiously. Once he
has disappeared as a source of gratuities—as a customer—his
body, his wife, and his daughter are rudely dismissed. Taken at
this surface statement, the story suggests only that, as Gorky
would have had it, Americans equal dollars. Once the dollars
cease to flow, Americans have no claim to courteous or even
humane treatment. (Here again there is the strain of caricature,
for presumably the Gentleman's widow would still have money to
spend.)

Such a reading leaves several aspects of the work out of account. If we look beyond Gorky and the simplifications of journalistic propaganda, the story becomes both wider and richer in
its implications. If, that is, we view the American Gentleman as
merely a part of the total narrative structure, Bunin's tale, while
still not subtle, is yet more ambitious and successful than preoccupation with the Gentleman allows it to be. To focus on the
Gentleman is to diminish fully a quarter of the work, for the final
fifteen pages, and indeed several passages earlier, move sharply
away from the Gentleman and his family. What we would
otherwise call background should here be seen as the center of
Bunin's interest. This background is round and fully drawn, with
careful and loving attention to the peasants and the natural world
that acts as setting for the Gentleman's travels, It is only the
Gentleman who is flatly caricatured—perhaps deliberately, so as
to direct our attention to the context which frames him.

The fictional modes of the story are curiously mixed. The
Gentleman is exaggerated satirically and the class which serves
him is rendered realistically, with humor or near-sentimentality.
And there are moments when the prose becomes distorted and
expressionistic. Here is a luxury liner:

Through the snow the numerous fiery eyes of the ship were hardly visible to the Devil who watched from the rocks of Gibraltar, from the stony gateway of two worlds, peering after the vessel as she disappeared into the night and storm. The Devil was huge as a cliff. But huger still was the liner, many storeyed, many funnelled, created by the presumption of the New Man with the old heart.[50]

"Stony gateway of two worlds" is richly ambiguous. There is America and Europe, but there is also the world of pleasure and luxury enjoyed by the ship's passengers and the feverish servitude of the menials who attend them. And there is the bright gaiety of the liner and the dark violence of the storm. This liner is, in fact—or rather in fancy—larger than the natural mountain. It suggests the presumption of civilization: it is "enduring, firm, majestic—and horrible." The overfed captain of the ship is likened to a pagan idol, and the descriptions of the microcosmic world inside raise the question whether the Devil would not be more at home within than without.

The same cosmic stage is evoked in the grand hotel—another pagan temple—and the desk clerk confronts the American Gentleman as if from a dream, a highly unrealistic nightmare of premonition. The Gentleman is clearly only the central figure, a useful foreground locus in a larger world Bunin means to attack. He is chosen as a likely, and ready-made, representative of modern civilization. Around him, entered through him and his wealth, is the empty Babylonian world of the pleasure ship and the big hotel. The Gentleman and all those he associates with treat their waiters and chambermaids as objects wholly devoted to the physical well-being of the people they serve. But just as natural law has its revenge on the family's overindulgence through the painful seasickness of the trip to Capri—and the final death-dealing stroke—so too it is the heretofore invisible serving class which becomes articulate and "endures" through the final quarter of the story. (It is this dismissal of an effete, insulated life which doubtless attracted D. H. Lawrence to Bunin's story and interested him in translating it). Bunin is an artist. He takes Gorky's American millionaire and links him with the liner, the hotel, and the devil himself to evoke "the New Man with the old heart"—the modern world Bunin seeks to contrast with the primitive energy of the storm and the peasantry.

The capitalist villain proved invaluable for many German satirists as well, and Brecht and Lion Feuchtwanger, to name only two, continued Frank Wedekind's practice of drawing models from America. In 1924 the *Berliner Tageblatt* began receiving doggerel verses supposedly written by an American and translated and submitted by a German. As more of the poems appeared, a portrait of Mr. B. W. Smith (roofing and kindred products) emerged which closely resembled George F. Babbitt. When Feuchtwanger admitted his hoax and collected the "ballads" in book form, he dedicated the volume to Sinclair Lewis. And he prefaced *Pep* (1927) with a note central to the present study: "If these poems, to some extent, are an attempt to put Babbitt into lyrics," Feuchtwanger wrote, "I certainly do not claim to be representative of America, a country I do not know. I wanted to hit at the European bourgeois, who more and more adopts for himself those characteristics which he likes to think are American, but which suit his own tendencies. In Europe today there are wide classes of people who are, perhaps, more 'American' than most inhabitants of the United States. It is this Americanism, not America, which is the subject of 'Pep.' Mr. B. W. Smith is less 'Homo Americanus' than 'Homo Americanisatus.' " [51]

In 1913 Bernhard Kellermann's *The Tunnel* signaled for Europe the growing distance between an America of Indians and mythic escape and one of technological advance. Kellermann's fantasy sold ten thousand copies in a single year. Thereafter no imaginary traveler to America could escape using the marvelous tunnel Kellermann built under the Atlantic; the romance of Cooper and Columbus was henceforth to yield more and more to the material wizardry of industrial know-how. And henceforth utopian visions would be less religious and political and more economic and technocratic.

The German technological novel reflects an interest in the increasingly intricate mechanization of modern society much like that inspired by the work of American engineers in the Soviet Union. A widely read novel by Hans Dominik, *John Workmann the Newspaperboy* (1909, 1921, 1925), combines a rags-to-riches immigrant story with a detailed tour through the intricacies of several American industries—and the construction of the Hudson River tunnel. The hero even works for Ford and comments on the conveyor-belt system; his stint in the slaughterhouses leads to a full report on Upton Sinclair's *Jungle.* Dominik was a graduate engineer and basically a technocrat. His interest in an efficient society led him repeatedly to an American setting (e.g., *The Steel Secret* in 1934 and *The Power of Heaven* in 1937). His most sympathetic characters are German scientists working for American firms; American businessmen usually exploit them with the help of marvelously skilled but frequently unimaginative American engineers. Gŭido Bagier, in his story of Edison and the early film industry, *The Resounding Light* (1943), repeats the view that America has the efficiency and energy to steal from others, usually Germans. Most of these tales appeal to local-color curiosity and simple patriotism, but Hermann Strenger's *A Stream from the Earth* (1942) makes a most creative use of technology and the dramatic possibilities of American industrial adventure. Strenger's materials are drawn from the world of oil and sulphur, but the technical detail—always interesting in itself—is never allowed to bury the human problems at the center of the novel.[52]

As I suggested above, only a few uses of American technology in the writing of the thirties transcend local color. And only a handful of these books have appeared in English. Valentin Kataev's novel *Time, Forward!* (1931-32) illustrates imaginative use of the American technician and is interesting enough in its own right to mention here. The plot turns on the construction foreman Margulies and the climate of progress inspired by the Five Year Plan. Margulies wants to break the record for pouring cement, and by the end of the book he and his crew succeed. Also involved in construction is the American businessman Ray Roupe—a sophisticated, remarkably cultivated reversal of Gorky's capitalist. It is Roupe who raises Kataev's fundamental queries about the quality and goals of the new Russian life. John Bixby is the American engineer who works closely with Margulies and encourages him to break with traditional limitations. Set a new record, he tells Margulies. "You are an enthusiast . . . ," Margulies replies.

"I an enthusiast? No, I am an American. . . ."
"But is it technically possible?"
"Technically, everything is possible." [53]

Margulies's admiration for Bixby's know-how is neatly figured in the engineer's "small aluminum notebook, which was also a pocket slide-rule." Margulies has dreamed "of having such a thing for a long time. It was amazingly convenient. On the spur of the moment, one could make the most complex calculations, including even logarithms. It was indispensable. Such was American technique!" [54]

Bixby is a good fellow. He learns Russian and works hard for his Soviet employers, but Kataev is careful to contrast him with the selfless servant of the people, Margulies. Bixby has come to Russia for money, just as he has worked all over the world to build a bank account which will mean success in America. He laughingly admits he aspires to the bourgeoisie. Kataev might have had him change under the warm influence of Margulies and Soviet life, but his Bixby persists in hoarding his salary and dreaming of the material luxuries life in America promises. This persistence permits Kataev a final comment on the superiority of Margulies, for Bixby's bank suffers reverses and will not release his savings. Crushed at the collapse of his hopes, Bixby gets so drunk he cannot save himself during a hotel fire. Margulies and the purer hopes of Russia—the new construction record—survive. Kataev's American materials have helped demonstrate a central premise of his novel: "Soviet Russia is following the footsteps of the United States," one of the characters remarks, "but it is beginning where America is leaving off." [55]

The poet Rainer Maria Rilke, however, never accepted the technocracy he associated with America, and so the United States remained throughout his career an emblem which drew together everything he believed destructive of human life and values. His life was a constant search for images, metaphors, symbols—often highly personal. His frequent journeys to other countries were part of his quest, not for the fruits of tourism, but for concrete embodiments of his soul's vision. Nations themselves became symbols. And America was the enemy, the modern world, the source of change and of much of "the suffering within us."

"I no longer love Paris," Rilke complained in 1913, "partly because it is disfiguring and Americanizing itself. . . ." [56] What once served him merely as an emblem of the exotic—similar to Tahiti or any other little-known place—soon came to suggest anything alien, foreign, hostile to the soul and to poetry. The prime offender is the machine, and when Rilke mentions America he means to condemn the wholesale mechanization that has transformed Europe and the life lived there:

> Machines will destroy all our gains, if we let them usurp us, lording it still, as they do, in minds they were made to obey; relentless they grind out the free-stones for building all plumbline and purpose, ousting the chiselling hand, its wayward and delicate play.[57]

I cite Rilke's hatred of the *Zeitgeist* and its relation to his theory of his art because his persistent Anglophobia was essentially an emblem for attitudes which played a central role in his creative life. In the seventh and ninth elegies, for example, the need for man to persist in the highest of human acts, to join the poet in transcending evanescence by fixing reality in the permanence of art, is worked out in an attack on modern civilization. "Nowhere, beloved, can world exist but within," Rilke insists in the seventh elegy. The next six lines evoke the threat the poet fears from "der Zeitgeist":

> where once was a lasting house, up starts some invented structure across our vision, as fully at home among concepts as though it still stood in a brain. Spacious garners of power are formed by the Time Spirit, formless as that tense urge he's extracting from everything else. Temples he knows no longer.[58]

Unlike Goethe and Mann, Rilke never came to celebrate the soul unencumbered by ancient memories and crumbling castles—a soul perfectly at home in the present. Once his position is recognized as a desperate defense of European traditions against the threats of depersonalized modern civilization, his use of America to embody the hated *Zeitgeist* resembles the polarization which lends dramatic shape to other modern European writing. America seldom appears directly in Rilke's poems, and yet it embodied metaphorically—as the poet himself realized—a major theme of his art.

Rilke was perhaps the most gifted, sensitive—and persistent —opponent of what he felt was the spirit of the time. What he called "Americanization," critics like Georges Duhamel would call "modern." Kellermann's tunnel had brought the technology of the west flooding eastward. Or, more precisely, technology was itself the tunnel, the means by which national, continental, and cultural boundaries have been dissolved into an ever more homogeneous present. "You are going to America?" Jean Cocteau once wrote Klaus Mann. "You'll see New York? It's like visiting a fortune teller." [59]

One of the most influential identifications of America's present with Europe's future was what Gilbert Chinard once referred to as "the too famous and misunderstood book of Georges Duhamel." [60] The misunderstanding is caught neatly in its English title, *America: The Menace.* For the translator and for countless readers, the book was simply a bitter indictment of American life, a life which had rankled the refined French sensibility of the author. But Duhamel was distressed by the English title. His own had been *Scénes de la vie future* (1930). America is being used, as Duhamel's Preface makes clear, as a metaphor. It "represents for us the future. . . . My arrows, passing through America, will hit the whole world. . . ." Like Tocqueville before him, Duhamel stands firmly on an older civilization he sees threatened by disintegration. And like the earlier visitor, he has chosen America as the most advanced model available for study. In effect, Duhamel anticipates the remark attributed to Harrison Salisbury after a visit to Los Angeles: "I have looked upon the future—and it doesn't work."

A similar use of America is made by Henry de Montherlant in *The Master of Santiago* (1945). Set in Avila about 1519, the play's central figure is an ascetic saint of denial committed to the service of Christ. Spain no longer recognizes a need for such holy service, and the chivalric order he leads is dissolving before the colonial ambitions of his country. As Montherlant presents it, Renaissance Europe is pursuing a future inimical to its medieval past; the emblem he chooses to suggest the new era is America. As the play opens, three of the knights announce their intention of seeking their fortune in the New World. Their departure will destroy the order. The Master himself has need of money, for his daughter wishes to marry but has no dowry. He is never really tempted, however; colonialism means for the Master—and for Montherlant—brutalizing greed that will corrupt and sap the strength of the mother country. A ruse to persuade him that the king recognizes the danger and requires his virtue abroad fails when his daughter responds to his integrity by sacrificing her betrothal and revealing the stratagem. The New World thus becomes simply "The World" which crushes the good unless they flee from it. In a mystical moment of climax, father and daughter rededicate their lives to Christ and to suspension in the Nothingness that will free them of the World. Their sole recourse is escape to monastery and convent.

Louis-Ferdinand Céline's remarkable and puzzling novel, *Journey to the End of the Night* (1932), illustrates more fully the use of America to evoke the quintessential modern world. "A novel of pessimism," in the words of an early admirer, Leon Trotsky, "a book dictated by terror in the face of life, and weariness of it." [61] Like much modern fiction, Céline's novel describes a journey, not only through life but into life. The hero, or rather, antihero, Ferdinand Bardamu, passes from youth to middle age, bouncing from the First War through army hospitals, medical school, lunatic asylums, African jungles, and a visit to America. The central location, however, is France, or perhaps even Paris at the Place Clichy; the repeated side trips are simply images of Bardamu's spiritual turbulence. The significant journey—and a de-

tailed and excruciating one it is, both for himself and for his
audience—is to the center of his life. Since he begins where
earlier travelers have stopped, since he sees life from the first as
Night, as Illness, as Hallucination and Death, we are not surprised that the fruit of his search is worse than mere nothingness—it is nausea. For Irving Howe, it is a "cheerful nausea,
a tone largely beyond bitterness or protest. . . . The material . . . is
frequently appalling, yet the voice of the narrator is not at all
what we have come to expect in the contemporary literature of
exposure and shock." Howe draws an instructive contrast with
Dostoevsky: "Dostoevsky's underground man trembles in
fright and despair before the possibility of nihilism; Céline's no
longer regards a valueless existence as anything but a fact to be
taken for granted." [62]

After five hundred pages and several dozen episodes, the narrator stops short in midsentence and snaps, "Let's hear no more of
all this." The very pointlessness of the novel's close and of so much
of the action is itself the point—Céline seems to say, "I've gone as
far as you can go, and there is nothing there." The novel is in
effect a morality play with Bardamu an Everyman for whom
everything always comes up tails. And yet the suggestion persists
that Bardamu is a willing scapegoat. If we watch his life closely,
for what actually happens to him rather than what he complains
of, we see that he is not remarkably unfortunate. He seems to
choose to be miserable, as if misery is a condition somehow free of
illusion and self-deception. Just beneath the surface of all Bardamu's complaints we feel his sense of responsibility, his willing-
ness to perform a task for the good of us all. "Off I went into the
night," he remarks repeatedly, and we are surely meant to bless
him for his courage.

Like every philosopher-artist, Céline had to discover ways to
objectify his metaphysics. He uses language which halts and reels
to suggest hallucination. There are descriptions of illness and
death to portray a life that is no different. Then there are the
travels themselves: into the army, to show human life as stupid
and incomprehensible; into the African jungle, to find it worse
than meaningless when naked of civilization. And then on to New
York and Detroit, with no attempt whatever to provide motiva-

tion. Why, we might well ask, does Bardamu go to America? What does his experience there help Céline to say?

He certainly has no need to take Bardamu such a distance to declare that modern science is meaningless. Bardamu is himself a practicing physician who repeats again and again how little he knows and how powerless he is. America is used by Céline not so much as an arena where science presumes to master nature, but as an effective setting for hallucination. Like Kafka, Céline makes of New York an expressionistic nightmare. There are long avenues of gigantic buildings, large hotels with interminable hallways (one is called, delightfully, The Gay Calvin or, as the original has it, in English, the Laugh Calvin), and ominous crowds which frighten Bardamu and refuse to acknowledge his existence. There is the meaningless employment he finally secures—an invention surely worthy of Kafka—picking fleas from new immigrants on Ellis Island and crushing the insects with his fingernails. New York is once more size, impersonality, and the impossibility of communication.

New York also brings Bardamu to the cinema—for the European of the twenties and thirties always characteristically American, and for the European artist a favorite emblem of modern man's spiritual sterility and diminished size. Duhamel's *Scénes de la vie future* (1930) contains a lengthy dramatized indictment of the American movies and their audiences. Duhamel notes a "hypnotic" condition in the people waiting to enter the theater. They are pushed forward, he writes, "like lambs going to slaughter." (Another patient crowd of moviegoers leads Duhamel to repeat the image later exploited so frequently by Brecht: "What was it that the slowly advancing crowd made me think of?" Duhamel asks. "Was it not the animals who mounted the incline to the slaughter?" [63]) The theater has "the luxury of some big, bourgeois brothel—an industrialized luxury, made by soulless machines for a crowd whose own soul seems to be disappearing. . . ." The movie itself is distressingly artificial. The life on the screen is imitation, "and who was to know whether that human multitude that seemed to dream what it saw, and that sometimes stirred unconsciously like a man asleep, was not imitation also. Everything was false." [64]

Most of Bardamu's interest in the movies is related to one or another of these observations. An additional element may have been drawn from Paul Morand's *New York* (1930). Morand's visit to the cinema resembles Duhamel's closely, but his apocalyptic hyperbole charges his vision with a fearfulness Duhamel's more direct attack never achieves. Morand writes: "A nightmare light falls from imitation alabaster bowls and yellow glass lanterns and ritualistic chandeliers; the organ-pipes lighted from below by a greenish glare, make one think of a submerged cathedral, and in the walls are niches intended for cursed bishops. I find a deep, soft arm chair to sink into, and for two hours I watch giant kisses on mouths like the creases of the Grand Cañon—embraces of Titans, a complete propaganda of flesh which, without satisfying them, excites these violent American natures. It is worse than a black mass, it is a profanation of everything: of music, of art, of love, of color. I could say that I have had a complete vision of the end of the world." [65]

This is Bardamu's American cinema too, but as always he accepts and indulges himself in the modern world which he re-viles. (In a French theater he compares to those in New York, he decides that Parapine's band of lunatics make a perfect audience.) "It was pleasant inside the [New York] movie house," he remarks, "warm, and comfortable. . . . Not a moment lost. You plunge straight into an atmosphere of warm forgiveness. You only had to let yourself go to feel that the world had at last become indulgent. . . . Then dreams waft upwards in the darkness to join the mirages of silver light. They are not quite real, the things that happen on the screen. . . . You have to hurry though to stuff yourself with these dreams, so as to get through life which is waiting for you outside, once you've left the theatre, so as to last through a few more days of this strife with men and things. You choose from among these dreams those that will warm your heart the most. For me, I must admit, it was the dirty ones that did. It's no good being proud, you've got to take from a miracle whatever you can hold." Céline's enthusiasm for the movies can be felt in the basic structure of his novels, while at the substantive level he returns again and again to the idea that "the cinema, that new little clerk of our dreams, can be bought, hired for an hour or two, like a whore." [66]

When Bardamu flees to Detroit from the nightmare world of

New York, the landscape narrows and becomes less cluttered —and perhaps all the more horrible. Céline brings his Bardamu from New York to Detroit to add a single nuance to his American metaphor. "I came," Bardamu says, "to a group of great squat buildings full of windows, through which you could see, like a cage full of flies, men moving about, but only just moving, as if they were contending very feebly against Heaven knows what impossibility. So this was Ford's. And then all about one, and right up to the sky itself, the heavy many-sided roar of a cataract of machines, shaping, revolving, groaning, always about to break down and never breaking down." Bardamu succeeds in getting a job—the examining physician actually seems pleased that he is an invalid: "In the job you'll have here," he says, "it won't matter what sort of a mess you're in." When Bardamu protests that he is an educated man, he draws a stern rebuke: "Your studies won't be any use to you here, my lad. You haven't come here to think, but to go through the motions that you'll be told to make. . . . We've no use for intellectuals in this outfit. What we need is chimpanzees. . . . We will think for you, my friend." "Look out," a fellow worker warns him. "Don't miss a day here, because if you do they'll throw you out in a jiffy and in another they'll have put one of those mechanical things in your place, they're always handy. . . ." [67]

Detroit gives Céline a unique opportunity—to show his worthless man actually being replaced by a machine ("They've got a machine-thing in your place now." [68]) And it provides the novel with its most nightmarish and at the same moment most contemporary sequence. The other situations are in a sense timeless: war, illness, death, lunacy. But with Detroit's machines Céline can suggest that things are not only terrible, they are bound to get worse. As we shall see, Kafka can hint that as an engineer his Karl might survive in a world of machines. For Céline the possibility of survival is never seriously entertained. With Detroit and the Ford Motor Company, he hit upon an image of utter hopelessness.

In Cesare Pavese's *The Moon and the Bonfire* (1950), Céline's empty world moves from America to Europe—and the ironies are heightened by other American imagery we have noticed in our discussion. Pavese's short novel focuses on a brief moment in its narrator's lifelong search for meaning. He has, in the familiar fashion of modern art, been seeking his identity. When we meet him he has come back to his small Italian village after twenty years in America; we watch his disillusionment develop and then we leave him as he returns to wandering.

The narrator was born, we learn, illegitimately. As a child he had no sense of home and was shifted about regularly on the charity of the villagers. As soon as he could he ran off to sea to escape what he felt was meaningless daily routine. We learn very little about his travels. He settled in California, worked at the wine trade he knew well, and seems ultimately to have become a successful bootlegger during Prohibition and a wealthy, respectable wine wholesaler afterward. But he apparently always felt himself an outsider in America—he was held as an alien during the Second World War—and so he has returned to Italy in search of his past, his people, his land, and himself.

"Even in the old days," Pavese writes in his Diary, "we referred to the 'hills' as we might have talked about the sea or the woods. I used to go back there in the evenings from the town when it grew dusk, and for me it was not simply a place like any other; it represented an aspect of things, a way of life." [69] It is this sense of place, this aspect of things, that the narrator seeks. He seems to feel that if he had stayed at home like Nuto—the carpenter who is the narrator's alter ego—if he had stayed in Italy his life would now have the shape and substance he longs for. But as his past is slowly unrolled in the sterile present tense of the novel, it becomes clear that each strand was predestined for decay. What with war, poverty, exploitation, and ordinary human weakness, all those he once loved have been destroyed. The life he remembers so fondly is now summed up for him in what he sees as the villagers' superstitious faith in the rejuvenating powers of the moon and the annual bonfires. He had never before been able to accept these myths of the soil, but until he does, his friend Nuto insists, he cannot become a "countryman." Not only can you not go home again, the novel seems to be saying, but it wouldn't have made any difference if you had never left.

Most simply of course, America in Pavese's book is the place his narrator went which was not Italy. It represents the wide world, being away from home, cutting roots. But the metaphor is far more intimately enmeshed in the novel's fabric than this. The narrator's California is distant from Italy and yet much like Italy: there is the climate and the wine trade, the large Italian population and the frequent encounters with immigrants from home. Yet it is a land whose life and people the narrator cannot understand. "I realized," he says, "that as far as I was concerned, the whole nation were bastards." "Where do these people have their home . . . ? Is it possible to be born and live in a country like this?" "These people were Americans and Mexicans, and Italians who seemed always to just have arrived, and they lived on the land in the same way as the streetsweepers in the city cleaned the sidewalk." [70]

The one place in California which shines most vividly in the narrator's memory is the desert. Because his truck had broken down, he was forced to spend a night alone in what he calls the "heart of America." He fell asleep in his truck, and then: "Later in the night a loud barking noise woke me with a start. The whole plain was like a battlefield. . . . There was a reddish light and I jumped down, cramped and stiff with cold; a sliver of moon was piercing the low clouds and it looked like a gash from a knife and bathed the plain in a blood-red light. . . . It terrified me." For him, he says, America was a slap in the face. "It was too big a country—I should never get anywhere. . . . The more places you see, the less you belong to any of them." [71]

America is cold, heartless, empty. But this is what he has found in postwar Italy. *The Moon and the Bonfire* is not a simple immigrant tale. It turns on fundamental human questions concerning life in the world of the twentieth century; its use of America resembles Kafka's and Céline's. But here the world of the future is not merely mirrored from abroad; it has arrived in Europe. There is literally nowhere one can go to be made whole. The hills of Italy have become indistinguishable from the deserts of America.

Pavese's statement is not quite so negative as Céline's, however. There is certainly no redemption in sight, but he is willing to entertain a possibility, however ambiguous. The narrator's story seems to pick up an echo in the young boy Cinto. He too is disabled from birth; in his case it is a crippled leg. Perhaps, through the help of the narrator and his friend Nuto, the boy's life can be made meaningful. Nuto, after all, believes in the renewal myths of the moon and the bonfire—and it is in the moonlight, as Cinto's cottage burns and with it his corrupt family, that the boy is adopted by the two men. Perhaps life may be rich in the smaller things: Nuto's modest humanitarianism for instance, or the intricate penknife that the narrator has given Cinto and which has brought him such joy. But what are we to make of the fact that the last we see of Cinto he has lost his knife and is rummaging about distractedly trying to find it? Perhaps the ingenious toy is Cinto's American adventure—and its loss may well suggest his participation in the rootless life that all modern men share.

Such a life, however, is not peculiarly American, nor is it a direct consequence of the spread of American culture. Pavese suggests more strongly than most European writers that "American" has come to mean "modern." "After several years of study," he remarked in 1947, "we comprehend that America was not another land, another historical beginning, but merely a gigantic theatre where, with more frankness than was possible anywhere else, the drama of everybody was being enacted." [72]

As these glances at Céline and Pavese illustrate, the modern world that is Europe Americanized will naturally include—or conclude—the persistently held American images from an earlier time. I should like to end this survey by citing a little-known but fascinating work which illustrates this point even more clearly while returning us to an observation I offered tentatively at the start. One reason the American metaphor now appears to have exhausted its possibility of growth is the thorough self-consciousness of its role in contemporary art. Yves Berger's short novel, *The Garden* (1962), makes an apt postscript for my investigation of America's metaphoric possibilities. Like Céline and Pavese, Berger modifies the traditional image of America as promised land. But where they merely dissolve its distinctness, Berger can be said to turn it on its head. *The Garden* is in effect a parody of Chateaubriand and the countless travelers and writers who saw America as Paradise. The narrator's father, a wealthy land-owner in the south of modern France, is persuaded that life was at its most nearly perfect in the plantation society of Virginia, in—as he so often says—"about 1842," "when we had just the amount of civilization we need." The father is a latter-day Henry Adams who measures the world's decline from this ideal moment. He has never seen Virginia of either the nineteenth or the twentieth century, yet he has made his estate a facsimile of a southern plantation, he dodges automobiles on asphalt highways in his horse and buggy, and he so manages it that the local movie house runs only American cowboy films.

He labors to pass his obsession along to his son and daughter. He even names his daughter Virginia, and thereby effects one of the novel's more curious ironies. The son moves from his father's dream of Virginia to the mortal flesh of his sister and then irrevocably back to the stable illusion of 1842. Virginia, as embodiment of paradise, lures her brother to incest in the hope of destroying the myth which threatens to paralyze him. She urges the narrator to commit his ideal world to book form, hoping the encounter with the concrete, with time, will free him from the endless circles of his dreams. The book she sponsors, we gradually realize, is the novel we are reading. To a remarkably great extent it is in fact composed *en Virginie,* but the style of the novel itself records her slim chance of winning her brother from the eternity of his myth to the temporality of her love.

The American myth of *The Garden* is ingeniously associated with an Emersonian theory of language. The father celebrates a primitive time when words were pure in their oneness with the things they denoted: here once again is the dream of stasis. The father builds careful sentences to trap his words and hold time still:

> Words which evoked bygone spectacles, forgotten traditions, buried rites, a ruined faith and these words fell from his lips into my visionary ears, fell warm and palpitating, opening on the evening gatherings, community prayers and meditations, choirs, ceremonious sarabands, the open-air banquets which used to follow visits from one farm to another, from one plantation to another, something like a carefree solemnity and it sometimes happened that, turning toward Vir-

ginia, toward me, my father would hold back his words swollen with pictures or would repeat them insistently, so that a flock of restless doves would flutter around my head and as he, the bird-catcher, pulled the thread attached to their feet, I would see, at eye level, between heaven and earth, in a lingering vision, girls such as the one my father wanted for me, demure in a crinoline, with an eager heart and the sort of modesty which is no longer to be found, those true maidens who, from their mothers and from fear, had learned the art of waiting.[73]

These lines illustrate the rich texture of Berger's art. For we are made simultaneously aware of the father's myth of Virginia, his effort to capture it verbally, his forceful transfer of it to his son, and his son's receptivity and pleasure in his father's linguistic creativity. (We come eventually to sense Virginia's potent presence in scenes like this—she does not see doves, nor is she a maid in crinoline prepared to wait while time stands trapped in the endless clauses of father and son.)

I want to pursue the matter of sentence structure further because it is not only central to the essence of the novel but plays a crucial part in the bare plot itself. This sentence follows closely upon the one I have quoted. It illustrates the transfer of myth from father to son and records as well the son's preoccupation with his father's *manner*:

... I remember my father's sentences when he started speaking, at first like a steady surge on which I rocked to and fro, then the sentence expanded, each new word filling it out and pushing it farther on, higher up and when it had reached that altitude at which I expected my father to gasp for breath, it arched its back in a fury and collapsed, huge, dislocated, digging a hole in its fall and I hurriedly tried to bury, so as to find them later on, some of the words which had splashed me, but then the sentence started again, rose again, soon becoming a whirlwind, a cyclone and in fact my father did not run short of breath, his sentences were like those fisherman's nets I have read about which stretch for

miles, hanging vertically, held by posts as my father's sentences were by commas, invisible posts, inaudible commas,
present supports, hidden supports and that, I believe, is the
secret of a narrator's art, a novelist's art and not long ago,
urged on by my sister, I myself tried to tell this story: Virginia before it changed, about 1842, and we know very little
about that perfection, an equilibrium between flora, fauna
and ourselves, then we had adequate weapons and men's
dreams were flagging but the emigrants took to the sea, crazy
hordes of covetous men who wanted nothing but to clear,
plant, build, invent, and push back the natural frontiers and
the tents became villages, the villages towns, and the towns
cities and I can see my father, every morning and again
before the other two meals, reading the shit from the original
text he translated word for word, from six to ten pages of the
American Notes on which he often commented sentence by
sentence so that the reading was always cut up, chopped into
pieces by commentaries longer than the passage itself and
after Dickens one day, it was Tocqueville the next, Le Père
du Poisson or Saint-Jean de Crèvecoeur, not to mention that
Frances Trollope whom my father hated as much as Dickens for her *Domestic Manners of the Americans* and whom, over
the years, he has as it were married to the Englishman,
calling her a shit too, I suppose because he could never think
of a feminine form of that word. Then we were at liberty to
begin lunch.[74]

The first sentence here moves from the father's involuted phras-
ing up to the book in hand, the novel Virginia has prompted the
narrator to write. He dutifully proceeds to the story of America
but then drifts toward his childhood and his father's obsession
with that story. He has moved in a circle; only rarely in the novel
is he able to pin himself to the march through time demanded by
the simple declarative statement about lunch. This is the kind of
sentence Virginia insists he use. She associates it with the necessary temporality of their affair and the health of human sanity.
She demands "full stops," while he yearns for "hooks on which
time is strangled." [75] She has arranged their love affair with the

hope that he can be won to her view. But at the level of plot the
sentences I have quoted signal her failure. They have been composed in Virginia's presence during one of the rare lulls in their
lovemaking. There are a few pages in the novel where the lines
shorten and the narrative moves briskly forward, but the flight
from time into the circularity of countless clauses gradually returns. When Virginia reads what her brother has written—and
sees *how* he has written it—she gives up the battle and leaves him.
The completed novel is itself circular and we last see the narrator
where we first met him: in the twilight of the plantation garden
reading and re-reading the book in which he has trapped time
and, through madness, escaped it.

The Garden is a remarkable novel, an ingenious prose tour de
force. As David Lodge has observed, "The fact that M. Berger
was awarded the Prix Femina for this, his first novel, restores one's
faith in continental book prizes." [76] Like Green, Berger is interested in the psychological fruits of obsession. America as Paradise,
America as Europe envisioned it for so many years, is an original
and imaginative fixation on which to focus. Paradoxically,
America is here associated with stability. The Virginia of 1842 is a
refuge whereby father and son escape time and change. Nothing
is said of modern America. And yet the civilization studied by
Duhamel in America surrounds the estate in France and presses
on Berger's extraordinary family. First the chemical fertilizers
used on adjoining fields kill the high-flying birds father and son
identify with, and then the father himself is killed when his buggy
collides with a speeding automobile.

The two Americas in *The Garden* had appeared frequently in
continental European literature. What is worth remarking in
Berger is the full articulation of his primitive America *as* a myth
and his picture of a modern world so unmistakably French; the
great success of his novel is due in large part to his recognition of
the fictional possibilities in the juxtaposition.

The comparison of Berger with Julian Green above suggests a
final comment before we examine the use of these images in some
of the most powerful writing of our century. Green goes further
than Berger in associating sexual perversity with America. Such
perversity offers fine material for the psychological novelist, but

where Berger introduces it into the lives of his French characters as an adjunct of insanity, Green and Soldati assume that the psychological twists of perversity they seek become readily available once their characters are made Americans. The source of such an idea—surely a curious one for the American reader (but obviously one easily accepted by his European counterpart)—might very well lie in the Menckenism of the 1920s and its identification of America's puritan heritage with Prohibition, the repressed sexuality of nineteenth-century gentility, and the hypocrisy of Comstock's censorship. Such at least seems to be Sartre's image of America in *The Respectful Prostitute* (1946).[77]

I will look more closely at this assumption during my discussion of Soldati and Green in the next chapter.

V

Six Writers

For after all what is a poetic revelation
if not basically the discovery of a new
world?
—Giame Pintor, "Americana"

Part One traces the genesis and growth of Europe's American imagery. In the previous chapter I have tried to enumerate the most important types Europe has created and to illustrate the variety and complexity of the uses modern European writers have found for them. My examples have thus far been drawn largely from individual works and authors not well known in the United States, and I have often kept them serviceable by narrowing the range of my comment and simplifying the density of the work to isolate the contribution made by its imagined America. The present chapter seeks to redress the balance tipped by this concentration. My authors include some of the most gifted, accomplished, and best-known artists of our century. In their hands, Europe's American imagery has often risen to full aesthetic integration, transcending the limitations of local reference to play a major role in their work—rising, that is, to the level of metaphor, a cluster of connotations recognized and felt internationally, freed from any necessary reference to particular time and place.

Such a judgment on my part requires more complete investigation than I have recorded to this point. By centering on a few writers I am able to examine the work and the man in greater detail; and where it seems helpful I have asked what personal, political, and historical elements have played a part in shaping his artifact and the America which has contributed to his success. I have looked, in sum, at important writers from Russia, Germany, Italy, and France, and I have asked why Mayakovsky, Kafka, Brecht, Soldati, Green, and Perse made such extensive use of Europe's America—what has it helped them to do and, as artists, to say?

Mayakovsky

Alexis de Tocqueville and Henry Adams were not the only nineteenth-century observers to note a kinship between the United States and Russia; Europe's enthusiasm for Franklin and Jefferson was echoed farther to the east. When Nicholas Chernyshevsky reviewed Tocqueville's *Democracy in America,* he accepted America as a model of political and social progress. The American Civil War attracted a great deal of attention in Russia, due partly to the enormous success there of *Uncle Tom's Cabin;* Lincoln's emancipation of the slaves had its counterpart in the freeing of the serfs in 1861. When the Russian writer introduced America or Americans into his work, he could depend on certain connotations: personal opportunity, crazy money, gold mining, endless prairies, wild Indians. He looked west for the materials of exoticism and for villains with a predictable effect on his readers. Maxim Gorky's failure to anticipate the power of American Victorian morality on his ill-fated trip to New York led to new possibilities for imagery. But as the modern era brought increasing industrial development to Russia the suggestive power of American materials was bound to change. America might be the home of greedy finance capitalism, as Gorky had pictured it, but its money managers had built a technological wonderland which the new Russians revered. Looking about him in 1913, Alexander Blok noted the changes coming over Russia. He recalled the old church ways, the travel by sleigh, the vast steppes, and the history of barbarous wars. But now a gradual transformation was beginning to assert itself; its agents were the factory chimneys and "black coal—subterranean Messiah!" The face of Russia had new eyes, "like a stranger's": [1] they belonged, we realize, to the western world, for Russia was becoming, as the poem's title suggests, the "New America."

Even in translation Blok's poem is an impressive artistic achievement. And it is prophetic as well. It draws upon the familiar conception of America as the future and develops the links between the two nations that many had seen. But it also anticipates by a decade a period of intense competition and cooperation as Soviet Russia strove to learn the secrets of American industrial success and engineers journeyed from the United States to share their technical skills. Communism's critique of American business success lost much of its persuasiveness when Soviet Russia—and the Europe which formed the audience for its propaganda—recognized its need for the very technology which supported capitalist wealth. As early as 1880 Dostoevsky could have a character refer to Americans as "marvellous engineers" and "good technicians";[2] by 1922 Ehrenburg can use Ford as a synonym for "the last word in modern technique" and locate Jurenito's fabulous mechanical transportation system in New York.[3] The first Five Year Plan specifically affirmed the need to surpass American industrial development. "We want to catch up with technical America and to outstrip it," wrote Ilf and Petrov in their popular American travelogue. "To catch up with America! That task which Stalin set before our people is immense . . . ."[4]

About five years before he was able to arrange a trip to the United States, Vladimir Mayakovsky made extensive use of America in his epic of revolutionary Russia, *150,000,000* (1919-1920). In an exuberant volley of some 150 lines, Mayakovsky depicts hand-to-hand combat between Ivan, a giant personification of 150,000,000 Russians, and Woodrow Wilson, champion of American civilization and an oversize replica of Gorky's millionaire. At stake is the course of the future. But although this is "the championship class fight of the world,"[5] Wilson and his America partake of all the ambivalence we have come to expect of their appearance in Russian literature.

Mayakovsky's poem is both a hymn of praise to the Revolution and a call for unity among the diverse peoples of his country. Come, he cries, let's all march together and "we shall find a new Russia." It is only with the cooperation of every citizen that Ivan can defeat our enemies, poverty and starvation. "Today, the eyes of the whole world are on us"; we must "busy ourselves with miracles." Acting as with a single will, the Russian people will succeed in creating a new world. This is, of course, the new America of Blok's poem, and Mayakovsky likens his Ivan to Columbus. Ivan will be like God in his creative power, and "America" is the land of promise he will fashion. This America is the technological wonderland of the visiting engineers, and Mayakovsky's images repeatedly echo the Futurist trust in a modern world made habitable by machines.

But America is also a specific nation whose capitalist empire blocks Ivan's path. While accepting the energy and enterprise which have made America master of the machine and brought it enormous wealth, Mayakovsky identifies America's culture with the crudest Philistinism. This polarization helps him stage his personified confrontation between "red and white": the time of compromise is past, "all middles are done away with," for the two hemispheres of the world have split apart and hardened. After his technology—including toxic bacteria—has failed to defeat the "radiant" Ivan, Wilson sends out "his last army—a poisonous army of ideas." Ivan defeats the archaic Roman law and the prods of heaven and hell which have held the people enslaved ("plots of superstition"). "The classics hid themselves in 'The Complete Collection of Works' as if in burrows," but "the futurists have routed the past, giving to the winds the confetti of culture." Next comes "the trash of the Louvre," and then Wilson himself is reduced to ashes.

> Trampling the corpse of the past with factories,
> the future bawls in trillions of trumpets:
> . . . .
> The future has come!
>   The future is the victor!
> Hey, you centuries,
>   Come take a bow!

Herbert Marshall has called Mayakovsky the troubadour of the Russian Revolution, but before Stalin sealed his fame with the famous declaration, "Mayakovsky was and is the greatest poet of our Socialist epoch," [6] there was considerable controversy over the nature and value of his achievement. Gorky was an early supporter,[7] but Lenin thought *150,000,000* "pretentious trickery" and "hooligan Communism"—"Rubbish, stupid, double-dyed stupidly . . ." [8] and Leon Trotsky dismissed the poem as nearly unreadable "Bohemian silliness." [9]

Trotsky cannot accept what seems to him Mayakovsky's egotism; this is at the base of his dismissal of *150,000,000* and his charge of Bohemianism. "At every step Mayakovsky speaks about himself, now in the first person, and now in the third, now individually, and now dissolving himself in mankind. When he wants to elevate man, he makes him Mayakovsky. He assumes a familiarity to the greatest events in history. This is the most intolerable, as well as the most dangerous thing in his works." The complaint has a familiar ring to American ears—the reckless poet who "has one foot on Mount Blanc and the other on Elbrus," whose favorite word is "shout." [10] Whitman too was criticized for singing a "Song of Myself" and for proclaiming verses (his "barbaric yawp") seemingly framed for public declamation. It is not often stressed in discussions of Mayakovsky that the Russian and the American resembled each other in more than their sprawling lines and passion for the vulgate. Mayakovsky's identification with the Revolution was as total as Whitman's union of his own voice with that of American democracy, and it is not unlikely that the former took the latter as model. "In 1915," Kornei Chukovsky recalls, "when I was working on my translations from Walt Whitman, Mayakovsky evinced considerable interest in his poetry. Mayakovsky was at that time very much impressed by the role of Whitman in the history of world poetry as a destroyer of Old Testamental literary traditions, damned by the 'many-headed louse' of Philistia. . . . Walt Whitman was dear to him as a forerunner." [11] Judging from his own self-dramatization as troubadour of the Revolution, Mayakovsky did not share the difficulty of early American readers in seeing Whitman's "I" as a conscious personification of national identity. Chukovsky, in fact, was amazed at how well Mayakovsky understood Whitman, apparently by pure intuition. He appeared to have no knowledge of the English original, yet he "divined it as unerringly and spoke of it with as firm an assurance as if he were himself the author of those verses." 12

Mayakovsky's fame was firmly established in Russia when he made his trip to Cuba, Mexico, and the United States in 1925. Because he so identified himself with the present and the promise of the future, he found use for America more frequently than any other writer discussed in this book (a possible exception is Bertolt Brecht). When Volume 5 of his *Collected Works* appeared in 1927, it contained some twenty-two lyric poems—the "American poems"—and *My Discovery of America,* an impressionistic prose diary of his three months in the United States. Although, unlike the earlier *150,000,000,* this work draws on direct experience of the United States; its aims, its effects, and its metaphoric uses of America remain remarkably similar to those apparent in the earlier long poem Mayakovsky had written before setting foot on the North American continent. This is an important point, for in this way a significant amount of the later writing escapes the limitations of local-color description. Mayakovsky remained thoroughly insulated from American life by his total ignorance of English.13 As an artist he was left free to let his imagination play over the phantasmagoria he encountered. Not too surprisingly, he saw mainly what he expected to see, what he knew he would see even before he came. For purposes of poetry, the images and connotations he had always associated with America remained intact.14

In *150,000,000* Mayakovsky had sought to unify his poem by focusing his hatred of the political whites, of Philistinism, and of capitalism in the gigantic caricature of Wilson, "Swimming in fat." But the other details of the poem resist such oversimplification, and most of his Soviet critics refused to accept his surrealistic images. They usually complained that anyone could tell that the poem's author had never seen Chicago or any American city. But Mayakovsky's tour brought him to Chicago, and he later boasted of reciting portions of his poem on street corners and impressing the citizens with his knowledge of their city. A guidebook description is fairly accurate, he observes, but not so close to the essence as Sandburg's "Chicago." The picture in *150,000,000,* however, is the most truthful of all.

Which is simply to say that Mayakovsky saw little in America to alter his expectations. During the voyage over he writes, "The ocean is an affair of the imagination. . . . To the right there is no land all the way to the pole and . . . on the left there is no land all the way to the pole, before you there is a second, completely new world, and underneath you Atlantis, perhaps. . . ." His first thought is a conventional one, precipitated by the poverty of Mexico: all the wealth of the hemisphere, including its very name, has been absorbed by the imperialism of America. But soon the boyhood dreamer preempts the party worker. His first anecdote reveals admiration for the Russian immigrant who has succeeded in America and at the same moment condemns him for becoming a dishonest capitalist opportunist. "By the word 'America' we understand a mixture compounded of O'Henry's eccentric tramps, Nick Carter with his inevitable pipe, and the checkered cowboys of the Kuleshov movie studio. There are none such at all." But the America the poet does see exists merely at another level of myth. "In the morning America was rolling by, the express was whistling, never stopping, taking in water on the run with its trunk. All around are the licked-up roads, ant-covered with Fords, some sort of constructs of technical fantasy." The entire country is for Mayakovsky a construct of technical fantasy, from the New York buildings which, Kafka-like, have tops he cannot see, to the brilliance of the all-night lighting that Gorky had wondered at, a prodigal waste of electricity which seems to Mayakovsky the epitome of thoughtless American wealth.[15]

The most interesting aspect of *My Discovery of America* is not that Mayakovsky should find America a technological wonderland but that, as Charles A. Moser has seen, the confrontation with the very machine culture he desired for Russia should fill the Soviet poet with so much uncertainty. The first shock comes from Coney Island, a nightmare sequence which surely owes something to Gorky, but which conveys a suggestion of Mayakovsky's own disappointment with the life his beloved industrialism supports. The inevitable blaze of light, the freaks, the ramshackle façades lead him to observe, "I have never seen any place where such a foul sight called forth such delight. . . . It must be that to lovers in New York the happy life seems to be just such an idiotic carnival." In Chicago, Mayakovsky's ideal city of mechanical efficiency, he encounters the stockyards. His description is lengthy and explicit, and he seems moved beyond the need for his customary hyperbole. (The entire scene reads like a preliminary note for Brecht's *Saint Joan of the Stockyards* and *In the Jungle.*) Here again the basic impression had been anticipated, by Zola and Upton Sinclair on the one hand and by popular European fantasies on the other. "People do not go through the slaughterhouses without its leaving its mark. When you have worked in them you either become a vegetarian or start calmly killing people when you are fed up with being diverted at the cinema. It's not for nothing that Chicago is the place of sensational murders, the place of legendary bandits." As his journal progresses Mayakovsky becomes increasingly aware of a dehumanizing quality in American life. He is stunned by the efficiency of the Ford assembly line: "There are no voices, no distinct rumblings. Only a general serious din. Greenish faces with black lips, just as during filming. This is from the fluorescent lamps." The scene anticipates Céline. For Mayakovsky the triumph of the machine has gradually become identified with the destruction of man: "At four o'clock I watched the outgoing shift at the Ford gates—people piled into the streetcars and went to sleep right there, exhausted. In Detroit there is the greatest number of divorces. The Ford system makes the workers impotent." Even in the apparent shock of direct observation, Mayakovsky echoes Gorky.[16]

America remained for Mayakovsky a metaphor for the life to be expected from technological progress, but his attitude toward that life changed. "The futurism of naked technology with the superficial impressionism of smoke and wires, which has the enormous task of revolutionizing the paralyzed, obese, ancient psyche—this elemental futurism has been definitely confirmed by America." There is no need for the poet to prophesy here, for this future can be transferred—is being transferred—to Russia. The task which confronts the artist is "not the hymning of technology but its control in the name of the interests of humanity. Not the aesthetic enjoyment of iron fire escapes but the simple organization of living quarters. . . . Perhaps the technology of tomorrow, multiplying the strength of man a million-fold, will proceed along the path of the destruction of construction, noise, and the other externals of technology."

There is thus a need for a "second discovery of America." The final lines of *My Discovery of America* catch the poet's ambivalence nicely. "We travelled to Paris. . . . In comparison with America wretched hovels. Each inch of land has been captured by agelong struggle, exhausted by the centuries, and used with pharmaceutical minuteness to grow violets or lettuce. But even this despised sort of little house, this little bit of land, this property, even this deliberate clinging for centuries seemed to me now an unbelievable cultural milieu in comparison with the bivouac-type set-up and the self-seeking character of American life. On the other hand," remarks the troubled futurist poet, "all the way to Rouens . . . we met a total of one automobile."

"Just you wait, bourgeoisie. There'll be New York in Tetushakh, there'll be paradise in Shuee." [17] How much Mayakovsky cherished America as a symbol is emphasized by his American poems. In "Cross-section of a Skyscraper," he rejects the life real Americans are living on various floors of the dwelling. "I look and I am filled with anger at those whom the building's façade hides. I travelled 7000 versts ahead and arrived seven years behind." In "100%," the poet describes the American of initiative and adventurous individualism he had expected to meet. "But I realized," he concludes, "that even I, a dissipated bohemian poet, was much more like this American fellow than the real American of to-day: there are no such 'guys' in New York." [18] When he was not complaining that the United States was unworthy of his idea of America, Mayakovsky attacked capitalism and predicted once again the triumph of Ivan over Wilson. Poems like "Broadway," "I Witness," "The Young Lady and Woolworth's," "Black and White," "Siffilis," and "A Decent Citizen" are fairly straightforward local-color adaptations of the American visit: "Bourgeoisie . . . your world-famous, streamlined America, for sure, we shall overtake and surpass." [19]

But with "Brooklyn Bridge" we once again encounter an artist's symbolic vision.

Give, Coolidge,
a shout of joy!
I too will spare no words
                about good things.
Blush
    at my praise,
                go red as our flag,
however
                united-states
                            -of
-america you may be.
As a crazed believer
                    enters
                        a church,
retreats
        into a monastery cell,
                        austere and plain;
so I,
        in graying evening
                    haze,
humbly set foot
            on Brooklyn Bridge.

After repeating his awe of the structure, "an austere disposition of
bolts and steel" where his "visions come to life," the poet praises it
as a perfect emblem of the modern world. If the planet should one
day be devastated and only the bridge remain,

        then,
                as huge ancient lizards
                                are rebuilt
        from bones
                finer than needles,
                                to tower in museums,
        so, from this bridge,
                        a geologist of the centuries
        will succeed
                    in recreating
                            our contemporary world.

This is what America would always mean for Mayakovsky, this "Bróoklyn Bridge—yes . . . That's quite a thing!" [20] If the existing political entity often resisted the myth, if "the American old woman of liberty waved her fist with its torch, covering the prison on the Island of Tears with her backside," [21] the poet could supply a remedy: "As for me, well I personally would like to close America, clean it a little and then discover it again, a second time." [22]

With the death of Stalin in 1953 and the ensuing cultural "thaw," the early America of prairies and gold mines gradually reappeared in Soviet literature. But Mayakovsky and the decades of technical aspiration seem to have made an irradicable impression on the Russian imagination. For two of the foremost poets of the next generation at any rate, America has meant primarily the technological future. Their use of these associations has been remarkably different, however, illustrating once again how intention and literary theory will dictate diverse purposes for similar materials.

"I have . . . an old dream—to write a book of poems about America." The kind of poems the young poet, Yevgeny Yevtushenko, may write can be seen in his "Girl Beatnik," "Monologue of the Beatniks," and "The American Nightingale" ("In the land of perlon and dacron, and of science that has become a fetish . . .").[23] Yevtushenko wants to describe America to his Russian readers and thereby contribute to increased understanding between the two countries. "I was in America for only three weeks and in a tourist-round saw obviously too little to write a book about. I would like to write about America at work—about American workers, farmers, intellectuals, and write it not from the point of view of a foreigner, but as it were from within. To do this, it will be necessary for me to come to the States once more —and this time to study it thoroughly."

Yevtushenko's friend and traveling companion on the American tour of 1961, Andrei Voznesensky, has returned twice—in 1966 and 1967. He has used this direct experience of the United States frequently, and yet his poems rarely turn on simple description. Both Yevtushenko and Voznesensky can be regarded as descendants of Mayakovsky, but where Yevtushenko resembles his public, social-realist side ("Poetry is savage war," he writes. "The Poet is a soldier" [24]), Voznesensky recalls the earlier Bohemian-Futurist. Herbert Marshall's comparison is helpful: "Yevtushenko's poems narrate, follow through a subject in a traditional way, attacking his object of criticism head on, using simple images. Voznesensky projects a montage of conflicting images and metaphors and allusions, without a narrative line or an overt connection; in other words, he is more subjective. . . . Party critics are still attacking Voznesensky for his 'obscurity' and 'murkiness' and 'subjectivity.' And indeed he compares himself to Joan Miro and his 'hypnotic paintings' and 'disquieting fantasy' and to Goya, of the 'Disasters of War' etchings. Yevtushenko's conception of the poet is as a soldier . . . but Voznesensky's poet is an 'accoucheur of the new. . . .'" [25] The ideas of rhyme of the two young poets help emphasize their differing conceptions of their craft: Yevtushenko insists, "There is one tool I never lay aside—that is old mother rhyme. However free the meter may be, old mother rhyme always holds it in check, so that it doesn't run wild. After all, the advantage of poetry over prose is in its retentiveness. I like certain unrhymed verse of other poets, nevertheless I must admit that unrhymed poems are much more difficult to memorize." Voznesensky, on the other hand, writes for "our young technical intelligentsia: there are millions of them in Russia now. Many of them work on enormously complicated machines—and they want poetry to be complicated, too. They have no use for rhymed editorials. . . . We're over-stuffed with rhymes: all fifth-form pupils make up wonderful rhymes. Our poetry's future lies in association, metaphors reflecting the inter-dependence of phenomena, their mutual transformation." [26]

There are sufficient references in Voznesensky's writing to attest his devotion to Mayakovsky. More significant than his complaint that Russia too often forces her best poets to suicide, however, are the frequent echoes of Mayakovsky's thought and technique: "The lilac tree glows like acetylene!" "All progress is retrogression / If the process breaks man down." [28] Mayakovsky's identification with Brooklyn Bridge informs Voznesensky's paean, "Mayakovsky in Paris." The poet discovers a picture of Mayakovsky chalked by a pavement artist on a bridge over the

Seine. "The crowds hurry over Your breast, the Seine surges under your spine. . . . A genius clinging to a bridge. You were Earth's ambassador. . . . Ah, how fatally You are missed! . . . Mayakovsky, You are a bridge," Your spine is "the aluminum flight of a bridge" between the early days of the Revolution and the present. "Thousands of stadiums shout to You: How're you thinking now? how're You breathing Comrade Bridge?" [28]

"Brooklyn Bridge" is the most successful poem in Maya-kovsky's American cycle: the Futurist poet merges confidently with the startling beauty of American technological achievement. Voznesensky's equivalent metaphor is the Kennedy airport,

> . . . accredited embassy
> Of ozone and sun!
>
> A hundred generations
> have not dared what you have won—
> The discarding of supports.
> . . . A glass of cool blue
>   without the glass . . .
> Brooklyn Bridge, rearing its idiot stone, cannot consort
> With this monument of the era,
> The airport.

As with Mayakovsky, the metaphor points to the poet as well: the airport is "the scion of a future that sports / Neither idiots / nor wedding-cake railway stations— / Only poets and airports!"

Voznesensky's vision, a future of poetry and physics, finds its symbolic reflection in America. In "A Beatnik's Monologue" he catches the contemporary fear of machines: "Machines as bar-barous as Batu Kahn have enslaved us men." They advance, the poet imagines, crying, "Meat! Human meat! . . . Give me your wife!" one says. "I have a weakness . . . for brunettes; I love them at 30 rpm." Our only recourse is flight, "into yourself, to the Church, to the john, to Egypt, to Haiti. . . ." When the cybernetic hallucination of "New York Bird" lands on his hotel windowsill, the poet examines it closely:

an aluminum bird;
in place of a body, a fuselage.

And on its corkscrew neck
like the tongue of flame
on a giant cigarette lighter
blazes
        a woman's
                face!
. . . the eyes like those of that girl somewhere
out in Chicago, face wreathed in cold cream. . . .

"Who are you?" he asks; "Perhaps you're the soul of America. . . ." [29] This particular rumination ends with a scream, but
Voznesensky as often tries to accept this vision, this soul of
America. "Some things are quite frightening, don't you think?"
he remarked to Anthony Austin in 1967. "This constant advance
of standardization, technology. It's not bad in itself: I use elevators, and my pants, like yours, have a zipper. What is bad is when
man, hypnotized by technology, becomes a technological object
himself." [30] Voznesensky's mystical faith in some future merging
of mechanical and human values leads to the chary affirmation of
"Italian Garage":

We were not born to survive, alas,
But to step on the gas.

But Voznesensky's use of America extends beyond that of
Mayakovsky and Yevtushenko:

Be discovered, America!
Eureka!

I measure, explore,
                discover, all out of breath,

In America, *America,*
In myself, *myself* . . .
. . . .

And if the poet's a hooligan,
Then so was Columbus—carry on!

Follow your mad bent—
                    head straight for shore . . .

You're looking for India—
                    look a bit more—

You'll find
          America!

Like St.-John Perse, Voznesensky has made effective use of
America as a metaphor of spiritual quest. He pursues his inmost
self through the subways of New York and down the alleys of
Greenwich Village. Though his eyes smart during a "terrifying"
striptease, he continues to watch,

          adoring and marveling, as
This downpour of woman responds to jazz.

"Are you America?" I'll ask like an idiot;
She'll sit down, tap her cigarette.

"Are you kidding, kiddo?" she'll answer me.
"Better make mine a double martini!" [31]

During his visit in 1967, Voznesensky revealed that he too is
planning an American cycle, to be called *Walkie-Talkie.* The first
poem has been published, and it suggests that he means to pursue
the existential question the stripper failed to answer.

Bless you,
Hugo,
Arthur Miller's dog,
a lovely creature.
You're not a dachshund,

you're a slipper,
a moccasin with a gaping sole,
shabby with use.

A certain Unknown Being puts you
on his left foot
and shuffles across the floor.
. . . .
Oh Hugo, Hugo . . . I too am someone's
    shoe. I feel the Unknown that is wearing me.

Earlier in the poem Voznesensky turns New York into a picture of both the vitality and the uncertainty so many Russian artists have associated with America:

Bless
        your big prick
at night Central Park
rank and thick as an instinct
        reeking of murder
you lie sprawled on your back
        between huge legs of stone—
what now?

The poet calls his world "a maximum-security prison" but insists that "still you must sing like a child." "America you're a rhythm," a rhythm Voznesensky will turn to poetic affirmation: " 'Long live everything!' For the art of creation is older than the art of killing." [32]

Kafka

The influence of Cooper and the romance of the American West prompted tales of adventure and escape in Germany as well as in Russia. And, as we have seen, Germans saw modern industrialism enshrined in America much as the Soviets did. But the possibility of actual migration from Germany to the United

States put resources at the disposal of the German writer un-
available to his Russian contemporary. As I have recalled in
Chapter II, large numbers of Germans actually did leave their
homeland and cross the Atlantic. As Harvey Hewett-Thayer observes, fifty to sixty years of immigration have guaranteed a
modern writer of his reader's interest, for "It may be said that
Germany has felt, through this indirect participation, . . . a kind
of proprietary concern in the great American experiment." [33]
This concern informs the work of Gerstäcker, Sealsfield, Ruppius,
Strubberg, Möllhausen—and the ubiquitous Karl May. But it
has inspired only one Franz Kafka and produced but a single
Amerika (1913, 1927).

Kafka's novel dominates European artistic use of the immigrant experience because he too sees Europe's future writ large in
America's present: America becomes for Kafka's Karl Rossmann
quite simply our world, and Kafka's persistent investigation of
the individual's plight in that impersonal world makes the immigrant experience seem a natural embodiment of his familiar
themes. If Karl is seen not only as yet another K.—another sur-
rogate Kafka seeking identity—but also as part animal (Ross/
horse) and thus typically human,[34] Kafka's personal quest becomes through his immigrant's story a metaphoric confrontation
between twentieth-century Everyman and his world.

If to the size and technical wonders emphasized in the engi-
neering tales we add the fantasy of *The Tunnel,* we have the basic
materials for Kafka's expressionistic representation of modern life
as more often than not a nightmare. Both the expressionistic
mode and the conception of America as a stage for Everyman's
modern journey lifts Kafka's novel above the concerns of local-
color accuracy. I want to examine it here with some care, not only
because it is an excellent example of a full-length use of the
American metaphor, but also because, like Gorky's sketches, it
contains many of the elements common to the works discussed in
the present study.

Kafka never visited America, and his friends were surprised to
learn he had written a book which employed it as a setting.[35]
Despite the outlandish buildings and distorted characterizations,
there is little in the novel to suggest the intense terrors of *The*

Castle or *The Trial*. Still, the first four-fifths or so do take place in what is recognizably the same world. It is the immigrant world of Karl Rossmann, and it retains a curious Old World ambience. Almost without exception, the most successful characterizations are European. Kafka's America is a melting pot, and while he could conceive of "pure-bred" Americans like Mack and Karl's English teacher (who, Karl assumes, is a millionaire's son), the vast lower stratum of American society—the level where Karl spends most of his time—is filled with people like Delamarche, Robinson, and the Manageress, first- and second-generation immigrants. The patrons of the Hotel Occidental remain mere suggestions, while all who concern Karl directly are given distinctive European characteristics.

This Europe-in-America is stressed from the moment Karl enters New York harbor with only his black traveling-box, an old army chest that makes a serviceable symbol throughout of his link with the past. Karl is the familiar immigrant in search of a fresh start, "a poor boy of sixteen"—the book begins—"who had been packed off to America by his parents because a servant girl had seduced him and got herself a child by him." (A few brief comic strokes like this temper the awesomeness of Karl's trials from the beginning and help ensure that the novel's tone will remain different from that sustained in Kafka's other writing.) Karl arrives in Kafka's America fully expecting prejudice and hostility, and he does not seem surprised by a Statue of Liberty which brandishes a sword. But it appears for a time that Karl may escape Liberty's assault; his Uncle Jacob undertakes his education and warns him of the pitfalls awaiting the unwary foreigner. Karl learns of the awe and bewilderment that often paralyze the newcomer and is cautioned to train himself carefully and choose a profession wisely so he will not be overwhelmed by his new experience.

Kafka's parable of survival is set against a backdrop of incredible, dehumanizing size. Everything that Karl sees is big: to his European eyes, America is a country virtually unlimited in geographic extent and material wealth. He forms a first and lasting impression of New York while still in its harbor. The countless ships from countless lands, warships sounding salvos, continuous

motion in every quarter—"A movement without end, a restlessness transmitted from the restless element [the sea] to helpless
human beings and their works!" [36]—this scene prepares Karl for
the city and its skyscrapers, with "their hundred thousand eyes,"
and for the ceaseless "doing business" which characterizes his new
home.

The implications of Kafka's exaggerated scale become even
more apparent in his extended treatment of "A Country House
near New York" and "The Hotel Occidental." Some distance
from the city stands the home of Mr. Pollunder, Kafka's approx-
imation of an American businessman.

> Like the country houses of most rich people in the neigh-
> borhood of New York, it was larger and taller than a country
> house designed for only one family has any need to be. Since
> there were no lights except in the lower part of the house, it
> was quite impossible to estimate how high this building
> was. . . .[37]

We never learn how high it is—though the sketch suggests infin-
ity—but it does not take long to realize that horizontally, at least,
it is a very large house indeed. With rooms fit for a ball and hints
of a chapel, it is no surprise to find, "as they passed along the
corridor, . . . at every twenty paces . . . a servant in rich livery
holding a huge candelabrum with a shaft so thick that both the
man's hands were required to grasp it." [38] To suggest, perhaps,
the endless sweep of modern business prosperity, the house is as
yet unfinished. (The insight seems lost, however, as the can-
dlelight sends long eerie shadows toward the countless closed doors
of the endless corridors; it is an American country house only in
name, for it is essentially another Kafkan castle.)

Kafka uses the same gigantic calipers on the Hotel Occidental,
where Karl takes one of the few jobs open to immigrant labor and
becomes a lift-boy. Located far from any city, this huge met-
ropolitan hotel is a self-contained microcosm, carefully com-
partmentalized to answer every need of its elite clientele. Karl's
hotel is served almost entirely by European personnel and main-
tains a continental atmosphere throughout, but there is no mis-

taking the detailed account of the information service in the lobby as Kafka's version of high-pressure "efficiency." Besieged by lengthy lines of questioners, two men sit in a glass booth and fire responses without a moment's hesitation. Served by a corps of pages who supply needed reference material, they resemble two disembodied heads, utterly devoid of personality. The point is made again in the book when automobiles roar out of the mist with no one, apparently, sitting inside.

Everything that Karl knows is metamorphosed in the new land, and nothing impresses him more than the intricacies of modern business. Kafka's desire to depict Karl's wonder leads to one of the novel's more charming absurdities. "There were no pedestrians, no market-women straggling singly along the roads towards the town, as in Karl's country, but every now and then appeared great, flat motor-trucks, on which stood some twenty women with baskets on their backs, perhaps market-women after all, craning their necks to oversee the traffic in their impatience for a quicker journey." [39] Kafka dwells on the size of American business enterprises, but the handling of Uncle Jacob, Mr. Pollunder, and Mr. Green transcends merely another chance to use the grand scale. Touring Uncle Jacob's building, where his uncle keeps ten separate offices for his own use and which would take "several days to traverse in its entirety, even if one did nothing more than have a look at each department," Karl says,

"You have really gone far. . . ."

"And let me tell you I started it all myself thirty years ago. I had a little business at that time near the docks and if five crates came up for unloading in one day I thought it a great day and went home swelling with pride. Today my warehouses cover the third largest area in the port and my old store is the restaurant and storeroom for my sixty-fifth group of porters."

"It's really wonderful," said Karl.

"Developments in this country are always rapid," said his uncle. . . .[40]

Kafka is not too sure just how these rapid developments are brought about, but he suggests some combination of "scandalous" recruiting methods that have made the firm "notorious throughout the whole United States" and the mechanical efficiency that plays such an essential part in the makeup of the "haves." Uncle Jacob is a man of principle and stern self-control, but his character has the inflexibility of a machine. He might well embody both Gorky's capitalist and the number of ambitious immigrants who rode to success on the backs of their fellow Europeans. At any rate, humanity is not one of his principles, for he throws Karl to the wolves—Delamarche and Robinson—without even a final hearing. If the brief glimpse we are given of Uncle Jacob's office routine is any index of him or any other American businessman, its cold and inhuman nature, comparable to that of the hotel's information booth, is a fierce indictment of efficiency and success.

For some reason neither seems fully to understand, Karl's visit to the country house displeases his Uncle Jacob, and Karl loses his sanctuary as fortuitously as he had gained it; he has indeed been "pulled under" by his new friend. A wedge has been driven between Karl and the past. The resulting journey brings America before Karl's eyes, the same kaleidoscope of impressions faced by any immigrant forced to find his new life in the new world. The stay with Uncle Jacob has actually been no more than a brief respite: Liberty's sword awaits Karl and he must face it. The initial sequence is an effective suspension of the narrative which permits Kafka to contrast European ways with a kind of people and a life not usually accessible to the newly arrived immigrant; henceforth Karl's observations must be made from without. With the exceptions I have noted, the succeeding episodes are fleeting and only tenuously related to each other. Kafka's familiar bureaucracy, the impersonal "others" who control human destiny, are not notaby active in *Amerika*. Their presence is felt briefly in the captain's cabin, in the hierarchy of officialdom at the hotel, in the marvelous steel desk, in the policeman whose initial command is "Show your identification papers." When seeking to project the workings of democratic process, Kafka can offer Karl only a distant balcony from which to view campaigning politicians. Evidently government by the people appeared in Kafka's imagination as an invitation for noisy, unruly masses to reduce public debate and responsible action to chaos and impotence.

When Gustav Janouch showed Kafka photographs of some constructivist pictures, Kafka said: "They are merely dreams of a marvelous America, of a wonderland of unlimited possibilities. This is perfectly understandable, because Europe is becoming more and more a land of impossible limitations." [41] Europe's impossible limitations motivate Karl's travels. And though often humorous, the prevailing image of Karl's inability to comprehend his twentieth-century world—his persistent incumbrance by the black traveling chest—is predominently pessimistic. But this dark vision, so familiar to readers of Kafka, is totally absent from the final section of the novel. The last episode departs significantly from all that has gone before as it does from Kafka's writing generally. It is fundamentally different, not in style, but in its attitude toward the future, and hence in its utilization of America. This same ambivalence has afflicted many writers who have tried to use the American metaphor, and it helps account in Kafka's case, I suspect, for his inability to unify or finish his book.

For his last adventure, Karl is heading west. He had decided, appropriately enough, to become an engineer, but now we find him enlisted in what Kafka calls "The Nature Theatre of Oklahoma." There is the same insistence on size: "The first day they travelled through a high range of mountains. Masses of blue-black rock rose in sheer wedges to the railway line: even craning one's neck out of the window, one could not see their summits." [42] But the immensity of America is now benign. The Nature Theatre seems an incarnation of the Myth of the Garden—the Second Eden—which has played such a large part in Europe's American Dream. Kafka's bureaucracy is here bathed in a religious glow. The sword of Liberty is sheathed, for Karl has found a welfare state where he can make a place for himself in the previously hostile world. There is little to remind him of Europe in this combined New Deal and monastic order; his black box is nowhere to be seen. Kafka seems now to feel that, like his Karl,

America and the world of the future will travel a road quite different from the traditional path of Europe, and even more than Wassermann, he approves what he sees. But the belated realization that America may not be Europe writ large after all, that perhaps European value-standards are no longer applicable, generates enough tension to pull the book apart. In terms of parable, the novel disintegrates not through altering its image of America, but—much more fundamentally—in shifting its tone, its basic attitude toward the modern isolation of the self. The final episode is itself unfinished, but to the extent that it promises peace for Karl it points to a contradictory—or, at best—developing vision in the author himself.

Brecht

Kafka was not the first to recognize that America was ideally suited to the expressionist mode, that for the European every facet of life reflected grossly and gigantically when transferred to New York or Chicago. The world of Karl Rossmann can be found piecemeal in Wedekind; and in the later work of Wedekind's admirer, Bertolt Brecht, that world plays a major role in a surprisingly large number of plays and poems. There is, however, no Oklahoma for either playwright, except by implication. Wedekind felt that the Americans had destroyed the promise of the New World; Brecht's dismay at the course of western civilization can be read in the bitterness with which he draws his America and equates it with everything gone rotten in Europe.

Benjamin Franklin Wedekind (1864-1918) was probably the only significant German writer to have naturalized American citizens for parents. His two brothers emigrated to the United States and Wedekind himself wanted to join them; he thought of himself as an American citizen. The brothers' experience abroad was distressing, Wedekind himself loved but lost an American girl, and the family home fell eventually into the hands of an American industrialist. These repeated contacts with America—most of them touching personal or family disappointment—often lend a referential or local aspect to Wedekind's use of America.

But there are numerous instances where specific reference gives way to metaphoric statement, where America is enlisted solely as a suitable ingredient in Wedekind's wider literary discourse.

Wedekind's attraction for a place where life might be renewed is complicated by his personal association of America with unhappiness. In *The Awakening of Spring, Pandora's Box,* and *The Torch of Egliswyl* the characters' failure to run away to America leads them to disaster. Those who do get to America, however, in *Fritz Schwigerling, Mine-haha,* and *Bethel,* are equally unhappy. This contradiction is embodied in *Keith,* where Wedekind's ingratiating swindler uses a lengthy stay in America to develop the confidence and flair he will need for his career in Germany. America can be used in Wedekind's attacks on European social ills: in *The Young World,* America serves to link female emancipation and free love—with a touch of approval for superior methods of educating children. In his most autobiographical play, *Hidalla,* the social-scientist hero fails to establish his organization for the breeding of perfect men in Europe; only in America does he meet with some success. But if Wedekind could draw on the archetypal promise of the New World, he also used Americans themselves as a dependable source of villainy. There is, for example, the Yankee life insurance agent who seduces Fritz Schwigerling's wife, the ruthless, money-hungry predator Wedekind repeats in Rudolf Launhart *(Hidalla),* Georg Sterner *(Oaha),* and Meinrad Luckner *(Schloss Wetterstein).*[43] These characters speak frequently of America, but like Feuchtwanger and Kafka, Wedekind's interest remains centered in Europe.

Wedekind believed that the stage should present "beasts of prey." His capitalistic *Raubtiere* are direct descendants of Gorky's capitalists, and they proved irresistible types for German satirists—among them one of the century's most influential artists, Bertolt Brecht. Brecht kept his eyes squarely on modern Germany and its problems, but what he saw there led him to use America in one way or another with surprising frequency. For *In the Jungle of the Cities* (1924) and *The Rise and Fall of the City of Mahagonny* (1927, 1930), America is little more than a Kafkan setting, a boundless, unfamiliar land where anything is possible. Unlike Brecht's Europe, its future stretches before it with promise, and its people, if not already giants, can yet easily be drawn oversized and oversimplified, for their lives and aspirations suffer no limitations. Brecht made somewhat different use of America in later plays. As his concern with evil focused itself on capitalism (he began reading Marx and Lenin in 1926), he came more and more to narrow and simplify his image of America toward Gorky's symbol for the violence and greed of the commercial classes. What had been in the earlier plays a deliberately un-defined America-as-somewhere-else, America-as-not-Europe, be-came later a handy emblem for a specific socioeconomic system. With *Saint Joan of the Stockyards* (1929), *The Seven Deadly Sins of the Petty Bourgeois (Anna Anna) (c.* 1933), and *The Resistible Rise of Arturo Ui* (1941), America is identified with capitalism and made to bear an impassioned indictment for all Brecht found awry in his Germany.[44]

Before glancing at the plays to examine Brecht's imaginative uses of America, I want to recall the elements in his dramatic theory which made exaggeration an important element in his work. Brecht's insistence on *Verfremdung* has been much discussed. He worked to alienate his audience from the stage action, to drive a wedge between the emotion of the spectator and the emotion projected by the actor, hoping to discourage passive identifica-tion—for Brecht anti-intellectual and hence subhuman indul-gence—and to induce forceful social action. Though after *Baal* (1918-23) he rejected the romantic self-absorption of the Expres-sionists, Brecht's pursuit of *Verfremdung* resulted nonetheless in anti-realist drama, plays which frequently suggest the technique of the German school by making deliberate use of distortion and by shunning the photographic realism of naturalist theater. Brecht's attacks on inhumanity and injustice were prompted by deep dissatisfaction with contemporary Germany, but to achieve what he felt was a necessary freshness and detachment he set his tales in a fantastic Soho, India, China, or America. He writes:

It must be kept in mind that the pleasure afforded by images of such different sorts hardly ever depended on the degree of resemblance between the picture and the object depicted. The pleasure was disturbed very little or not at all by in-accuracy or even extreme improbability, so long as the in-accuracy had a certain consistency and the improbability remained of the same kind. The illusion of a story that developed convincingly, an illusion created by all manner of poetical and theatrical devices, was enough.[45]

Brecht found a fruitful setting in the city of Chicago, and he used it in three of the five plays we are considering here. (Chicago was also the setting for an unfinished study of a wheat king, *Joe P. Fleshhacker of Chicago.*) The Chicago of *In the Jungle of the Cities* (1924) serves well as another version of Kafka's large impersonal modern world. Or perhaps it is even more like Céline's: "In such cities you can't see from this house to the next," one of Brecht's characters says,

> You don't know what it means to read a . . . newspaper. Or to . . . buy a ticket. When people have to take these electric streetcars, they perhaps get . . . Stomach cancer. Without knowing it.
> . . . .
> You walk the streets with your children. . . and suddenly you're only holding the hand of your son or your daughter in yours, while your son or daughter themselves have sunk over their head in quick-sand.[46]

Brecht's only experiment with "absurd" theater deals with what is now a familiar theme: modern man's inability to communicate with his fellows. He posits a "boxing match," a fight without motive, a psychic battle to establish contact if only through conflict. "In the end," Brecht remarks, "the fighters themselves saw the fight for what it really was, pure shadow boxing. They could not come to grips even as enemies."

Brecht's heavy debt to Upton Sinclair's *The Jungle*—available in German from 1906—is apparent in his very first attempt to use an American setting. The Chicago of *In the Jungle* is little more than a fresh serving of Sinclair's city, with a heavy seasoning of gangsters and cheap hotels.* Garga, the clerk selected by Shlink (called

* In *The Political Theater* (1929), Erwin Piscator notes the impact Alfons Paquet's *Flags* (1923-24) had on Joyce, Dos Passos and Brecht; the play deals sympathetically with the Chicago strike of 1886 and probably influenced Brecht's *Saint Joan.* Eric Bentley suggests Rim-

"The Chief" by hoodlums like Worm and Baboon) as a worthy
opponent for the contest, looks out his window and comments:
"Ninety-five in the shade. Noise from the Milwaukee Bridge.
Traffic." Later we learn that the city is windy and apparently
near the sea, for "the lobsters are mating" and ships leave the pier
regularly for Tahiti. More significant is a simile employed by
Garga's mother. "Four years in this city of iron and dirt," she says,
"we wait like cattle in the stockyards." [47] Sinclair's novel opens
with livestock moving along runways to inexorable slaughter and
pauses to consider the aptness of the picture as a representation of
human existence. Sinclair's metaphor was bound to attract a
writer like Brecht who felt that human misery was inevitable in a
world dominated by injustice and greed. (There is even, in *Saint
Joan*, a character who falls into a vat and is sold off as bacon. Cf.
the slaughterhouse imagery of Zola's *L'Assommoir*, 1877, especially
the first and last chapters.)

Sinclair works his opening figure out in terms of an immigrant
family which has come to Chicago seeking employment, only to
be ground to pieces bit by bit in the great meat-packing machine.
Brecht's background for the struggle of Shlink and Garga is
similarly, though less completely, drawn. Garga's family has
moved to Chicago from the "plains" or "savannas" to the south,
but they long for their home in Ohio. "We were driven to the
city," Garga says, "but we have the faces of the plains." [48] There
are those for whom the city is too cruel, who go away, perhaps
"back to Ohio," but most are trapped. There are also the few who
succeed. Shlink, like Karl Rossmann's uncle in Kafka's *Amerika,* is
one of the few successful immigrants:

Garga: Did you inherit this house . . . ?
Shlink: No.
Garga: You worked forty years?
Shlink: With tooth and nail. I only took off four hours for
        sleep.
Garga: You came here poor?
Shlink: I was seven. I have worked ever since.[49]

---

baud's *A Season in Hell* (translated by Brecht's friend Theodor Däubler in
1917) and the Chicago setting of J.V. Jensen's novel, *The Wheel* (1905).

But Garga has not been equally successful, and as Shlink gains advantage of him in their mysterious match, he thinks of running away to San Francisco, to New York, or to the idyllic tobacco fields of Virginia. "I want you to come south with me," he tells his mother. "I'll work there. I can fell trees. We'll build a log cabin and you'll cook for me." [50] Such a picture is akin to Garga's dream of escape to Tahiti. Eric Bentley feels that Brecht was perhaps not serious in suggesting that the voyage could be made directly from Chicago; it seems more likely to me that the geographical error is a deliberate intimation that Garga has as much chance of finding a new life, of escaping from machine civilization to primitivist paradise, as he has of sailing from Chicago to Tahiti. Garga's father makes the same point at the play's close when he calls to his son: "Goodbye, Garga! Take a good look at New York. You can come back to Chicago when they're at your throat." [51]

In the final scenes of the play Garga sends a letter to the police—referred to throughout as "the Sheriff"—accusing Shlink of rape. The letter is made public, and it raises a howling lynch mob. Despite Shlink's contempt for the authorities—"I . . . could explain many things to the Sheriff as niftily as Standard Oil could explain its tax declaration" [52]—he is forced to flee to the shores of Lake Michigan, for Garga, now playing the able private investigator, has alerted taxicabs at every corner to be on the lookout for the fugitive. Shortly before his death Shlink utters the sad burden of the play. "If you stuff a ship with human bodies till it bursts," he tells Garga, "there will still be such loneliness in it that one and all will freeze." [53]

Chicago provides a persuasive setting for Brecht's parable; its exotic flavor for a German audience, its immense size and chilling impersonality give the struggle of Shlink and Garga the very cosmic scope Brecht seeks. In *The Rise and Fall of the City of Mahagonny* (1927, 1930) the target is the damage done to man by his own avarice and lust. And the setting is again the city—always for Brecht the cesspool of human depravity—this time a mythical city in Florida called Mahagonny (Mähägonny), or "the city of nets." Reminiscing some thirty years after the opera's first performance, Lotte Lenya recalled many of the elements that went into its make-believe picture of America:

All of us were of course fascinated by America, as we knew it from books, movies, popular songs, headlines—this was the America of the garish Twenties, with its Capones, Texan Guinans, Aimee Semple MacPhersons, Ponzis—the Florida boom and crash, also a disastrous Florida hurricane—a ghastly photograph reproduced in every German newspaper, of the murderess Ruth Snyder in the electric chair—Hollywood films about the Wild West and the Yukon—Jack London's adventure novels—Tin Pan Alley songs. . . .[54]

Each of these ingredients plays its part in the fabulous world of Mahagonny. The founders of the city are close kin of Baboon, Worm and the hoodlums, prostitutes, and pimps who people most of Brecht's plays. From *A Man's a Man* (1924-25) we meet again the Widow Begbick, the founding mother of the new city of nets. In the earlier play she resembles a public utility:

> In Widow Begbick's travelling bar
> You can smoke and sleep and drink for years on end.
> From Singapore to Cooch Behar
> Begbick's beer wagon's your friend. . . .[55]

With the help of Trinity-Moses, Fatty the Bookkeeper, and Jenny the prostitute's six girls, Begbick sets about building a city of sin where she can provide much the same service as before, this time for the newly rich miners taking gold "farther up the coast." The merging of the two coasts persists throughout, but again geography has no effect on pointedness of insight: "You'll get the gold more easily from men than from rivers," Begbick observes; "Therefore let us found a city here . . . like a net which is put out for edible birds." The net will be baited with gin, whiskey, girls and boys, and at its center will stand the "Here-You-May-Do-Anything Inn" (in another version, *Das Hotel Zum Reichen Manne*).

The new city is soon operating at full capacity. Jenny and her girls arrive, and sing in English the famous "Alabama Song," a haunting, bluesy foxtrot:

> Oh, show us the way to the next whisky-bar!
> Oh, don't ask why, oh, don't ask why!
> For we must find the next whisky-bar
> For if we don't find the next whisky-bar
> I tell you, we must die! *(3 times)*

The same urgency informs the next two verses in which the girls ask the way to "the next pretty boy" and "the next little dollar." Kurt Weill's music underlines the empty desperation of the plaint with a jerkily oversyncopated imitation of American jazz, matching the girls' hollowness with snare drum, banjo, and saxophone. Weill's contribution to Brecht's ironies is nowhere better illustrated than in the song's refrain:

> Oh, moon of Alabama
> We now must say good-bye
> we've lost our good old mamma
> and must have whisky
> oh, you know why.

This is the familiar lament of the decadent for the irretrievable past—here less a place than a happy state, if not of innocence then at least of steady employment under "mamma's" wing. Brecht intends criticism of the girls' bathetic self-pity, and Weill comes to his aid with a masterly parody of the popular American love song. In sharp contrast to the syncopated verses, the refrain carries the complaint of the prostitutes in a slow and sentimental dance tempo, brilliantly emphasized by a saccharine trombone solo.

The men who arrive to populate Mahagonny are essentially the same as the girls who have come to serve them. All are dissatisfied with the complexity of their lives; all seek renewal in the promise of primitive simplicity. As projections on the back of the stage show many figures moving toward what is now a large metropolis, an exchange between some newcomers on the one hand and Fatty and Moses on the other helps explain Mahagonny's attractions:

Men: We live in the cities. Below them are sewers; in them
is nothing. . . . We perish quickly and slowly they
will perish too.

Fatty: Here in your cities the noise is too great, nothing
there but unrest and dissension and nothing upon
which one can rely.

Moses: Because everything is so evil.

Both: If San Francisco burns, whatever you consider good
in it, behold, that too goes finally down the same
drain. Come to Mahagonny where the trains do not
pass, the golden city, gilded skins, golden tobacco.

"In the next few days," a loudspeaker announces, "the discontented of all the continents were on the move to Mahagonny, the golden city."

Before long, all restraint disappears from Mahagonny, as Brecht turns his invented American city into a nightmare of license and debauchery. Jake eats himself to death, all pretense of affection disappears from lovemaking, and Alaska-Wolf-Joe, representing intellect, guile, and cleverness, succumbs to raw brute force in his boxing match with Trinity Moses and dies amid laughter, savage cheering, and the noise of a brass band. (Much of this is anticipated in Wedekind's *Bethel*.) In a wild drinking scene, Jim is forced to pay the price for his anarchy, for he breaks the only law yet honored in Mahagonny: he fails to pay for his drinks. His friends will not help him, and Jenny shows the quality of her love with a refrain that echoes through much of the opera:

> For as you make your bed, so you will lie;
> There's no one to cover you there
> And if someone's going to kick, it'll be me
> And if someone's getting kicked, it'll be you.
> . . . As long as you grow older everyday,
> You don't care a rap about love;
> Then you got to make use of the short time that is yours.

As Jim is tied up, Moses announces his crime to the other customers:

> Hey there, people, there's a man who cannot pay his bar
>   bill.
> Impertinence, folly, and vice! And the worst thing is: no
>   dough!
> Naturally, this is a hanging crime, but, gentlemen, don't
>   let this interrupt you!

Jim's trial is a savage attack on justice in commercial society, figured in a caricature of the American courtroom. With Moses, the prosecuting attorney, acting as barker, the spectators pay five dollars for their tickets and file into a tent, where they lounge about reading the newspaper, chewing gum, and smoking. In the day's first trial, Tobby Higgins is accused of premeditated murder, but, while Moses delivers a set speech on the horrors of the crime, Tobby reaches agreement with the judge, Begbick, on the bribe that will free him. When Fatty calls, "Who is the injured party?" Begbick remarks, "If no injured party comes forward, we must perforce acquit him," and the spectators intone, "Dead men tell no tales." Jim is then arraigned and turns to his friend Bill for money to bribe the judge. "Jim," Bill replies, "I feel close to you as a person, but money is something else again." Unable to provide the bribe, Jim is sentenced to two days for encouraging Joe to fight to his death, two years suspension of civil rights for upsetting peace and harmony, four years at hard labor for seducing Jenny, and ten years in the dungeon for singing forbidden songs of joy during a hurricane. "But," adds the Widow

> because you did not pay for your three bottles of
>   whisky. . . ,
> You are sentenced to death, Jimmy Mahoney
> On account of lack of money, which is the greatest crime
>   which exists on the face of the earth. *(Wild Applause)*

One version of the opera has Jim face the chair of execution—actually onstage—with understanding of his failure: "The friends I bought were no friends, and Freedom bought for money is no freedom. I ate and was not satisfied, I drank and became thirsty." But sometime after the 1928/29 version appeared, Brecht deleted this to have Jim conclude:

I hope that my horrible death will not deter you from living exactly as it suits you, without worrying. For I too do not regret that I have done whatever I liked.

. . . You are one with all the beasts and afterwards comes nothing.

Earlier in the opera, we see what happened when God came to Mahagonny and damned its sinners: "All of you, go down to hell! Put your Virginia cigars in your bags!" "On a grey morning," the men of Mahagonny reply,

> in the midst of whisky, you come to Mahagonny.
> . . . In the midst of whisky you start this fuss in Mahoganny.
> . . . Everybody is going on strike. By our hairs you can't drag us into hell, because we always were in hell. . . .

This is Brecht's modern man, and it is not surprising that he turned to the Florida coast for his Eldorado of depravity—where Ponce de Leon sought the fountain of youth, where the jaded pleasure-seeker looks for a return of youthful enjoyment by escaping to the simplicity of the tropics. Such simplicity is as unattainable in Mahagonny as it is in Garga's Tahiti. For the sated businessman and the sated culture the answer is the same: it is only the artificial stimulation of decadence that offers any respite.

Brecht's drama gains in impact from the music of Kurt Weill. The primitivism of American jazz echoes the pretended simplicity of Mahagonny, but since the simplicity is only pretended, the music, like the pleasure city itself, becomes sophisticated parody. Every ingredient in a Brecht production works independently of every other. Weill's music can frequently be found underlining Brecht's strident lyrics, as in the "Alabama Song," providing saccharine themes for saccharine statement, but just as often it will contribute its share to *Verfremdung* by working artfully in contrast, often supplying religious pomp or sentimental lyricism for brutally harsh and acid dialogue: the music alienates itself and makes comment on the action. But however independent he may be in individual scenes, Weill's total vision consistently reinforces Brecht's. Taken whole, the opera comes much closer to

using America as a universe dominated by evil than does *In the
Jungle,* and it thus leaves us far better prepared for the virulence of
Saint Joan, The Seven Deadly Sins, and *Arturo Ui.*

Brecht's disillusion with modern capitalist society is nowhere
better rendered than in "Vanished Glory of New York, the Giant
City" (1929).[56] Although the poet clearly assumes Europeans in
his audience, the thurst is so direct it can hardly be called metaphoric—unless Brecht is chiding America for succumbing to its
own myth:

> Who among us still remembers
> The glory of New York the giant city
> In the decade after the Great War?
> America: fabulous pond!
> God's own country!
> . . . Like everyone's boyhood friend, incapable of
>   change!

Here is the melting pot assimilating all races; here is the Golden
Age; here is a people incomparably blessed, who travel "never-
ending roads," erect gigantic buildings at unparalleled expense
and think poverty a sin.

> What self-confidence! What a stimulus!
> The engine-room! The biggest in the world!
> Motor factories carried on birth-propaganda,
>   built autos ahead of schedule
> For the unborn!
> . . . .
> What men! Their boxers the strongest!
> Their inventors the most practical!
> Their trains the fastest!

This is the America Europe emulated: "We insisted too on
full-cut suits of rough material / With padded bulges at the
shoulders. . . ." American values and mannerisms, American
chewing bum (Beechnut) and comic-strip characters (Pokerface)
spawned apprentice businessmen and Regular Guys. "Oh, how

we aped the glorious race that seemed predestined / To dominate
the world by making it march forward!"

But for Brecht and his fellow Europeans there came a time of
disenchantment, "for one day there ran through the world a
rumor of incredible breakdowns.... Now it has got abroad /
That these people are bankrupt, / We on the other continents
(yes, also bankrupt) / Look on it all quite otherwise [than we
did]—we think more acutely." What about the tall buildings?
"We look at them more coolly. / What contemptible barns,
skyscrapers that yield no rent! / Filled so high with poverty ...
piled to the clouds with debt." And what of those speeding trains?
Now people say of the passenger, "He journeys nowhere / With
incomparable speed!" The promises of the American Dream, like
the vaunted machines, "are lying in giant heaps (the biggest in
the world) / And rusting / Like those over here (in smaller
heaps)," and the people are left "holding tight to their smiles
(nothing else!) retired world champions...."

In one of his antiwar poems Brecht wrote:

> Gang law is something I can understand.
> With man-eaters I've kept up good relations
> I've had the killers feeding from my hand.
> I am the man to save civilization.[57]

One reason Brecht was drawn toward communist ideology resembles his interest in America as a useful symbol: like Gorky,
Mayakovsky, and countless other artists, he was attracted by a
simplification of complex problems that would make them
available for direct literary juxtaposition. In communism Brecht
found a logical systemization of his world-view, a convenient
ordering of his thought that gave him a sense of direction and
purpose for his work. Artistically, the conversion could not have
been simpler. When Brecht joins the Left, Eric Bentley observes,
"all he has to do is rename his jackals Capitalists." [58] Responsibility for the cities, implied in *In the Jungle,* is now clearly linked
with industry. In *Saint Joan,* America and its capitalism are no
longer peripheral, for the play's very stuff is Chicago, the stockyards, and the packers, and its aim is to attack capitalist ethics

and their degradation of man. In place of a far-away land where human passions reign untrammeled, we find now the center of the capitalist world where all the evils of the system exist in grotesque and exaggerated forms. For a communist these evils find their expression in the class struggle; in his late plays Brecht is a good deal more careful in delineating this struggle than he had been earlier. *Mahagonny* portrays a corrupt commercialism, but its sinners come wholly from the laboring classes. (Red critics have not been slow to point this out and to damn the play as useless; it has never been fully accepted east of Berlin.) Like many intellectuals, Brecht had little firsthand experience with the proletariat—when workers appear in his plays they are most frequently oversimplified caricatures unlikely to satisfy communist critics or convince anyone else.* But his goons and vipers make very satisfactory capitalists, and so he turns Sinclair's Chicago upside down: the dispossessed retreat—not always entirely innocent—into the background, an undifferentiated mass. In their place we find the owners, the manipulators, the giants of industry, and those who share their values and ambitions.

The meat kings of *Saint Joan of the Stockyards* (1932) bear names like Criddle, Lennox, Slift, and Pierpont Mauler, "giant of packers, / Lord of the stockyards." [60] As a result of Mauler's war with Lennox, seventy thousand workers are out of work, work that has brought them only a bare subsistence:

> For a long time now this work has made us sick
> The factory our hell and nothing
> But cold Chicago's terrors could
> Keep us here. . . .
> By twelve hours' work a man can't even
> Earn a stale loaf and
> The cheapest pair of pants.[61]

* The Soviet playwright and novelist, Sergey Tretiakov, complained that in *The Mother* (1932), "the workers are hard to distinguish from each other; this is a general shortcoming of all Brecht's plays, which shows that he does not know the proletarian milieu intimately (this is a warning to him that he must get to know it so)." [59]

They are being treated "like Steers," they protest in the familiar Sinclair figure. The workers' only friends are the communists, who try to organize a strike which will force the packers to act justly, and the "black Straw Hats," a group like the Salvation Army which ministers to the poor with sermon, song, and soup. Joan Dark, at the head of the Straw Hats, fails to see that her message of patience actually protects the packers from the more violent remedies of the communists. "In gloomy times of bloody confusion," Joan announces,

> Ordered disorder
> Planful wilfulness
> Dehumanized humanity
> When there is no end to the unrest in our cities:
> Into such a world, a world like a slaughterhouse—
> Summoned by rumors of threatening deeds of violence
> To prevent the brute strength of the short-sighted
>   people
> From shattering its own tools and
> Trampling its own bread-basket to pieces—
> We wish to reintroduce
> God.[62]

But God is not what the workers want. In a daring attempt to alleviate their hunger Joan goes directly to Mauler, who is attracted by her innocence. While he negotiates the total collapse of the packing industry to secure a corner on all available livestock, he gives Joan money for the workers and arranges for her education in the depravity of the poor, hoping thereby to demonstrate the pointlessness of her sympathy. "Mankind's not ripe for what you have in mind," Mauler tells Joan. "Before the world can change, humanity / Must change its nature." [63] But even after a tour which reveals worker after worker willing to sell his brother for a more secure position, Joan will not abandon them: "If their wickedness is beyond measure, then / So is their poverty. Not the wickedness of the poor / Have you shown me, but / *The poverty of the poor.*"[64] (As Mack says in *The Threepenny Opera,* 1928, "First comes the food, then come the morals.")

Mauler's business maneuvering is more successful. With the

help of bribed politicians and mysterious "New York influences" which lurk behind long scenes of intricate stock market manipulation, he at last holds the city of Chicago "by the throat." For seven days 100,000 workers mill about in the snow and biting wind outside the now-closed packing plants. When Joan decides to join the workers in protest, she asks, "Are there no people here with any enterprise?"

A worker: Yes, the Communists.
Joan: Aren't they people who incite to crime?
The Worker: No.[65]

But as an army of police approaches with cannon and machine guns, it becomes apparent that the communists will precipitate violence. Watching the struggle develop, Joan comes to her first understanding of the capitalism she has beeen defending:

> I see this system and on the surface
> It has long been familiar to me, but not
> In its inner meaning! Some, a few, sit up above
> And many down below and the ones on top
> Shout down: "Come on up, then we'll all
> Be on top," but if you look closely you'll see
> Something hidden between the ones on top and the ones
>   below
> That looks like a path but is not a path—
> It's a plank and now you can see it quite clearly,
> It is a seesaw, this whole system
> Is a seesaw, with two ends that depend
> On one another, and those on top
> Sit up there only because the others sit below,
> And only as long as they sit below;
> They'd no longer be on top if the others came up,
> Leaving their place, so that of course
> They want the others to sit down there
> For all eternity and never come up.
> Besides, there have to be more below than above
> Or else the seesaw wouldn't hold.
> A seesaw, that's what it is.[66]

And since only violence can upset such an arrangement, Joan dissociates herself from the Straw Hats, a convert to atheism well on her way toward communism. As for the Straw Hats, their sellout is now complete: "Just give us a band and some decent soup / . . . and God will settle things / And all of Bolshevism, too, / Will have breathed its last." "And ever 'tis a glorious sight," the packers chant, "When soul and business unite!" [67] (The words recall the fusion of religion and finance in Gorky and Ehrenburg.)

The play ends with one of Brecht's finest ironies. Loudspeakers announce worldwide economic catastrophe: "Pound crashes! . . . Eight million unemployed in U.S.A.! . . . Six million unemployed in Germany! Three thousand banks collapse in U.S.A.! . . . Battle between police and unemployed outside Ford factory in Detroit!" while Joan dies slowly of the pneumonia she caught in the yards. But as she tries to proclaim her new insight into the economics of captialism—that there are two worlds which cannot communicate with one another, that "only force helps where force rules" [68]—her failing voice is drowned in the singing of the newly allied Straw Hats and packers who hope to exploit her sanctity by turning her into the patron of their renewed effort to enslave the workers.

In *The Seven Deadly Sins of the Petty Bourgeois (Anna Anna)* (*c.* 1933), a simple dance drama, the Chicago of *Saint Joan* expands to include the whole country, north and south, east and west, as an emblem of crass vulgarity. Working together for the last time, Brecht and Weill achieved a folk tale whose biting satire and jazz figures secure an immediacy of impact beyond the reach of their more subtle efforts.

As the ballet opens, Anna I stands at a blackboard with a pointer to trace the journey she and her sister have taken to earn money for a new family home. "My sister is beautiful, I am practical," sings Anna I,

> She is a little crazy, but I have a good head.
> We are really not two people, but only a single one.
> We are both named Anna, we have one past and one future, one heart and one savings account. . . .[69]

"One of the two Annas is the Manager, the other the artist," notes

Brecht; "one is the saleswoman, the other the article sold." Back in Louisiana behind the framework of a house which rises slowly as the girls surmount the dangers which beset them, the family sings a pompously moralistic hymn asking God's help for Anna II, who is a bit too easygoing and may lack the diligence necessary to success. After repeatedly intoning the Calvinist dictum, "Idleness is the beginning of all vice," they conclude with a prayer:

> The Lord enlighten our children that they may know
>   the Way that leads to Prosperity.
> May he give them the Strength and the Joyfulness that
>   they do not sin against the Laws which make us rich
>   and happy!

It appears that Anna II's idleness is not the only vice the family has to fear, for each city the girls visit offers its own temptation. Time and again Anna I must rebuke her sister for lack of dedication and purpose. When Anna II substitutes a serious dance for her scheduled strip-tease, she is accused of pride; when she attacks the ringmaster who mistreats her horse in a "Douglas Fairbanks type film," she is belabored for her anger; and when her dancing is threatened by overeating, she is condemned for gluttony. "They want no hippopotamus in Philadelphia," her sister warns, "they stand by their principle; 110 pounds is what we bought, 110 pounds is her value."

The climax of the girls' adventure occurs in Boston, where they have found a man who "paid well . . . for the sake of love." Anna I does her best to promote this love-bargain so reminiscent of *Mahagonny,* and when her sister falls in love with Fernando, a gigolo, she warns her that "unfaithful, your value is cut in half." Anna II is so incensed at finding her sister and Fernando together discussing the problem that she creates a scene: "She shows her little white behind, worth more than a little factory, shows it free. . . ." Love that brings no profit, she is warned, is merely lust.

At last the girls' efforts are crowned with success: the home in Louisiana is complete and their family awaits their return. But Anna II is beset by one more temptation, envy, the seventh deadly sin, whose attraction is suggested by a powerful march. The "triumph over Self" has taken its toll; she envies whoever is idle, proud, and not for sale, "raging at every brutality, giving in to his own desires, . . . loving only the Beloved." Anna I is again equal to the task of controlling her sister. "Eat not and drink not and don't be lazy," she sings, "think of the punishment which is the cost of love! Think what would happen, if you did what you pleased! Youth passes quickly, take no advantage of youth. Sister, believe me, you will see at the end that you will at last emerge in triumph."

These lines of Anna I emphasize the theme of this final scene: The last shall be first. Turning Scripture upside-down is one of Brecht's favorite forms of parody. Here he has followed the Protestant Ethic to its absurd and unchristian conclusion: in a capitalist society, what makes money is right, all else is vice. Once given the end which the girls pursue, it is only through conquest of much that is fresh and natural—above all, what is human—that the goal can be reached. And the moment the distortion is attributed to capitalist values, the ballet fits easily into a Marxist schema.

In *The Resistible Rise of Arturo Ui* (1941), Brecht turned once again to Chicago as an easily managed microcosm, placing within its limits and those of nearby Cicero all that he hated in the capitalist world. It is true that his play deals primarily with the triumph of fascism and the civic lethargy that makes it possible, but equally significant is the role assigned to decadent capitalism as unwitting contributor to fascist dominance.

In *Arturo Ui* Brecht sought *Verfremdung* in two ways: he not only recreated the Chicago of Al Capone and countless gangster movies, but he also underlined his exotic setting with blank verse, rhymed couplets, soliloquies, even characterization and staging, borrowed from Shakespeare. The object of Brecht's attack was the recent rise to power of Adolf Hitler, but to achieve freshness and immediacy for his all-too-familiar story, he transformed Hitler into an American gangster, Arturo Ui, *Gangsterchef,* and made his supporters Italian mobsters: Ernesto Roma (Ernst Röhm), Emanuele Giri (Göring), and Giuseppe Civola (Goebbels). These figures act out a simplified comic allegory of Hitler's rise to power that points the finger of blame at those who could have resisted it.

The play opens with a projection of headlines which tell the story in outline, an Elizabethan dumb-show, and a prologue which introduces the major figures. Here we first meet Arturo Ui:

> The hero of our show . . . king of the rod.
> Richard III seems like his next of kin.
> . . . The king of murderers he is.

"What you see tonight is nothing new / . . . written only to divert you," we are told. "Europe is witness to the play we show / These gangster characters are men you know. (Sound of machine gun fire. . . .)" [70]

Chicago is suffering an economic crisis. The leaders of the huge cauliflower trust—Flake, Caruther, Butcher, Mulberry, and Clark—are meeting to lament the trucks piled high with produce that roll daily into a market where customers buy "half a cabbage and that on credit." Arturo Ui offers to force the purchase of vegetables. "Tommy guns and pineapples," Mulberry remarks. "New merchandising ideas at last . . . a sure way to get new blood in artichokes." A more appealing possibility would be support from Dogsborough (Hindenberg), the highly respected "chairman of the grand old party." But Dogsborough must be approached carefully, for he is honorable, "pompous as a deacon," and quick to insist, " 'Gentlemen, Chicago is no pork barrel.' " "The city / Isn't stone and steel to him or someplace / Where people live and fight for food and rent. . . ."

When we see Arturo Ui with his henchmen we discover that his visit to the trust was an attempt to find work for his organization; his men are getting stale from inactivity, and—even worse—the fickle public is turning to new heroes. Fame is fleeting, Roma observes, and must be won over and over again. "Nineteen years ago," Ui recalls in a delightful parody of the American success story, "just a Bronx boy out of work, I hit this town / And got my start and if I do say it / I've been going places"; from a modest beginning with only seven gunmen, he has risen to the command of thirty. To help him with his plans for the future, Ui hires a destitute Shakespearean actor—"I played Antony in Zenith in

1908"—to teach him to walk, stand, sit, and talk in the grand style needed to impress the "little guys" when he moves into politics.

The cauliflower trust succeeds in corrupting Dogsborough and seems well on the way to recovery with public funds, but Ui discovers the arrangement and demands a share of the profits for his "protection": "I'll plug anyone who tries to touch a hair on your white head," he promises Dogsborough. With a murder on the city-hall steps and a spectacular warehouse fire, he convinces the trust that his services are indispensable. What chance the law has of impeding Ui's rise is savagely rendered in the trial of one of his gunmen for the warehouse fire—a trial essentially the same as the one in Mahagonny. When Giri establishes as alibi a hike he took to Cicero where fifty people recognized him, and his henchman is acquitted because "he isn't the type to set anything on fire, he's a baritone," a drugged lush named Fish is sentenced to fifteen years for the crime. The Counsel for the Defence (Dimitroff), the only honest participant in the mock trial, sounds the play's theme when he pleads for someone to stop Ui's march, but the only fruits of his protest are threats from Ui's hoodlums.

With the treacherous murder of Roma in a replica of the St. Valentine's Day massacre, Ui's power is consolidated, and he has the entire city under his control in less than two weeks. Expansion is now in order, and in a lively parody of the garden scene from *Faust*, Ui woos Betty and Ignatius Dullfeet (Dollfuss). When we next see Betty Dullfeet she is attending her husband's funeral. In a scene recalling *Richard III*, Ui succeeds in winning Betty's consent—not to marriage but to his providing protection for the grocers of Cicero. A few broken windows and damaged supplies convince most of these grocers that they, too, need Ui's organization. They are asked to vote on the issue, for Ui will move only through true democratic process. One grocer asks if he may abstain and is given permission to leave the meeting, but the ensuing gunfire speedily convinces the rest to support Ui's proposal. Again we hear the lament that someone must stop this gangster, but again no one is willing to assume the responsibility. Fresh from his triumph in Cicero, Ui looks forward to extending his influence to the major cities of the country and finally coast to coast, "wherever there are grocers."

In an epilogue, Brecht makes his concern even more explicit, warning: "Don't forget—/ The womb that spawned that thing is fertile yet!" The womb is most obviously indifference, but there is no denying the responsibility of capitalism. Slipping into decay—from the Hegelian point of view—and turning to fascism for support, capitalism is directly responsible for the otherwise resistible rise of Arturo Ui.

The changes which appear in Brecht's uses for America between *In the Jungle* and *Arturo Ui* illustrate once again the rich connotations available to the modern European artist. At one point or another America served Brecht as surreal setting, as credible locus of human depravity, as image of a modern world gone socially and politically awry, and as a source of circumstantial details—characters, situations, institutions—that provided the furnishings he sought for his plays. As his needs altered, so did the aspect of America he chose to evoke. The result was the fullest exploitation of the American metaphor by any writer of the period.

Soldati

Mario Soldati lived in the United States for two years. His youthful picture of New York, *America, My First Love* (1935) and Emilio Cecchi's more negative *Bitter America* (1938) helped shape Italy's image of the United States through the Depression and war years as Gorky's had already influenced Russia's for several decades. Soldati originally planned to emigrate. There were visits in 1929, 1932, and 1933, and although he remained in Italy, his interest in America persisted and eventually bore fruit in a major novel, *The Capri Letters* (1954).

Both Cecchi and Soldati were puzzled by American sexuality. Cecchi's assessment was the familiar one: "Puritanism sees in the sexual urge above all the peril of the flesh and an invitation to vice. . . ." [71] But when the young Soldati finally held a blonde beauty in his arms, her unsettling innocence led him to an elaborate theory he seems never to have abandoned: "The Anglo-Saxon women . . . see in the Negro an incarnation of guilt, and approach even the Mediterranean races, the Spanish, French, and Italian, with an obscure sense of sin. In the kisses of their own tall blond men they savor the perverse innocence of childish and familiar love; in the kisses of dark emigrants they fear—and covet—the male force of the adult and foreigner." [72] One would be hard put to find a more suitable comment on the remarkable novel he wrote some twenty years later; we might merely want to add this from the book itself: "Evil . . . is never in others. It's always and only in ourselves who desire it." [73] The second observation points to the theme of *The Capri Letters;* the first suggests —once Soldati has chosen sex as his neutral arena—the rich shades of good and evil he associates with his two American characters.

Soldati's tale is a simple one of a man and two women, but it is rendered extraordinarily complex by the way it is told and by the insistent self-imposed debasement and guilt of the two central figures. A fourth character, the ostensible narrator, Mario, introduces us to Harry Summers and Harry's Italian mistress, Dorotea, and he provides some important comment on the action as he understands it. But the bulk of the story is rendered directly in an autobiographical scenario Harry sends Mario with the hope it can be sold to a film producer. It is through this scenario that we come eventually to know Jane, Harry's American wife—first as she seemed when Harry married her, then as she emerges in the six letters she wrote from Capri; the letters are quoted as part of Harry's script. And finally, through Harry's eyes and the narrator's—and gradually through our own—we come to know Dorotea. In a tale where narration is almost the only subject, Dorotea remains elusive; she meets the narrator only three times, and we must take her character and motives at second and third hand. But at the close of Soldati's novel, it is Dorotea who prevails. It is her story that has provided the center after all, the center around which Harry's scenario has turned unwittingly from the beginning.

Although the narrator has not told Harry, he has had little confidence that anyone can "make a film with characters whose psychology was so complicated and exceptional, not to say unbalanced." [74] As the novel opens, Mario meets his old friend Harry Summers in Rome. Harry is tired and pale, "uncombed and unshaved, as I'd never seen him before and never thought he would look. On his delicate, almost adolescent chin were scattered little blond hairs. Something seemed to have happened to him." [75] Mario sees Harry as a typical foreign intellectual who chooses to live in a seedy artist's studio rather than endure the routine awaiting him at home: he has taught art history at an American university and lived most of his adult years in flight from the academic life of New York and Philadelphia. Late in the book, Harry echoes the adolescent motif himself: "I'm not a man. I'm an aging, selfish, complicated, cowardly adolescent, just sentimental enough to adore my children and follow all the tender traditions in which I've been brought up; cynical enough to put my own pleasure first, if my pleasure was to flout my children and tradition." [76] As we come to see from the scenario Harry writes for Mario, his pleasure—and this is what Soldati regards as American—does depend upon the flouting of obligation, tradition, duty. He has to feel debasement, the sting of a violated conscience, or he soon tires. Harry claims to have become almost totally European, but the Italians in the novel, even though they can never know him deeply, always think of him as American and urge him to solve his financial problems by returning home. The book depends upon our agreeing that only an American could cherish Harry's obsessions and complicated approach to sexual contentment.

The object of Harry's obsession through the six years spanned in the novel is the peasant woman, Dorotea. Here is Harry's description of her: "tall, heavy, imposing in her flashy clothes, a low-cut tailor-made or a white dress with red flower designs, her hair drawn back and gleaming, her forearms loaded with big gold bracelets, her long nails, her painted mouth and eyes, her patent-leather shoes, her aggressive walk, her brazen look. . . ." [77] What makes Harry's attachment singular is that it feeds upon outrage to the Presbyterian proprieties of his youth. "Not for a second have I ever deceived myself on her account. I'd realized from the first moment that she was a prostitute. And a prostitute she remained for me, even when I decided to live with her. For years . . . I always avoided being seen around in her company . . . because I realized how obviously she looked what she was, and felt ashamed of being seen beside her, even by people who did not know me. . . . Now I've reached the point of exploiting my own feelings of shame, and almost enjoying them." [78] He insists upon her vulgarity and cheapness. She is to him, in short, everything that he is not. He turns her, as he says, into an inscrutable idol, redolent of the mystery and primitive vitality his own country lacks. When Soldati embraced his blonde Texan in Brooklyn, he hoped to capture his American myth in the flesh. It is simple turnabout for Harry with Dorotea: he makes of this peasant in Rome the American dream of sinful, delicious Europe.

Harry's descent to Dorotea is by nature cyclic; he must go back to his office, his scholarship, his middle-class friends if he is to enjoy returning to her. Not only can he not marry her and let respectability spoil their relationship, he consciously seeks a wife who seems her opposite. When he first meets Jane, "At once I felt an extreme tenderness, almost pity, for her. She seemed so small, fragile, and nervous, so intelligent and suffering, so much in need of protection; and I felt urged toward her from the beginning by an arid, sad, sincere, yet inevitable feeling, which reminded me of my affection for my mother and which had about it, absurdly, a bitter flavor of duty; not the sweet one of love, nor the intoxicating one of pleasure. . . . *It was my duty to find her attractive.*" [79] Here Soldati draws on the tension he had found in Americans: the "obscure sense of sin" associated with dark-skinned races, "the perverse innocence of childish and familiar love" shared by compatriots. Without being fully conscious of it, Harry means to have both. Looking at "her small, thin, nervous body, the image of weakness and unhappiness, . . . I realized that she did not attract me; but I realized too . . . that the very fact that she did not attract me might . . . have its own attraction. The possibility suddenly opened in front of me in all its perversity and risk. The only women who have ever attracted me are tall, heavy, and coarse. Now I gazed at Jane's thin little body . . . and I said to myself, yes, perhaps there was some enjoyment to be got out of her—the enjoyment of trying the very thing that did not attract me, and enjoying it *just because* it did not attract me." [80] By dwelling on Jane's slight physical attraction, her Philistine background, Catholic religion, and what he takes to be her coldness and

conventional reticence in lovemaking, Harry creates Dorotea's
opposite, a "duty" he can enjoy despite the inclination of his
appetite and then violate to give his visits to Dorotea greater
flavor. "Perhaps," he muses, "it was the almost schematic contrast between them of sacred and profane love." [81] "Very often
the thought of Dorotea was itself enough to lead me toward
Jane; or the thought of Jane to lead me toward Dorotea." [82] Once while leaving Jane during the war, he recalls, "my
sorrow was strangely mixed with impatience; it was like a harsh
and intoxicating cocktail of two ingredients that strengthen each
other by their very mixing: one ingredient was sorrow at separating from Jane, the other impatience to be with Dorotea as soon
as possible." [83]

As Harry says, man needs both happiness and unhappiness. He
does think in terms of "schematic contrast": "Rome always urged
me toward sin; America toward chastity; Paris toward a compromise with both." [84] And although repeated shifts in time and
elaborate narrative variation make his story less schematic than I
have done here, his sense of his life does lend itself to easy for-
mulation. But while this account of his relationships may claim
most of the book's pages, it in no way represents Soldati's novel. It
is precisely because Harry's version of reality is distorted that he
retains our interest. He is so wrong while feeling so confidently
right about the women in his life that his whining dissatisfaction
at the book's close can only be comical. Harry the schemer has
been outsmarted after all.

Our suspicion that Harry sounds more in control of his affairs
than any man can possibly be is confirmed as circumstances
gradually bring Jane's story to light. She never appears in the
foreground, at Mario's level of narration. We see her only through
Harry's scenario and the letters he quotes. The irony which Harry
never fully sees is that her life has been almost a duplicate of his
own. Her "Puritan" background has made her a fit object of
Harry's sacred duty, but it has also brought her the same peculiar
needs that he has. When he first meets her and decides she is too
proper to make love before marriage, she is actually involved in a
passionate affair with Aldo, a "handsome Italian" who is everything her American values tell her to despise—and thus a rich

source of perverse sexual pleasure. Jane has been using Harry precisely as he has been using her. "From the very first moment I met you, Harry, I saw you . . . as a sort of living reproach for my relations with Aldo, a call and a hope to free myself of them. I think I loved you just for that. For you carried me up with you into your world, among your pictures, studies, thoughts, where everything is beautiful and pure. . . ." [85] This is certainly not the Harry we have come to know, but the implication is clear: it is as near the truth as Harry's idea of Jane. Soldati can sketch Jane's story more economically than Harry's because the two situations are so similar: there is the same cyclic movement from the cool austerity of dutiful marriage to the maddening pleasure of what seems degradation. And there is the same delight in conspiracy and the hidden self. "He's such a good man," Jane writes of Harry to Aldo. "And he suspects nothing, absolutely nothing, about me. I might almost say he doesn't know me." [86]

We have some opportunity to decide for ourselves about Aldo. He seems very much the young opportunist and part-time gigolo, reminiscent, perhaps, of Ruggero in *The Passion of Rosa* though less hard, selfish, and basically evil. As far as we can tell, Harry's assessment is accurate: "Aldo believed himself to be sly, cynical, and calculating, and always promised himself to bring off a master stroke some day, [but] in reality he was a nice, rather shy and rather lazy boy, who'd never been tough or persevering enough to profit from any situation by carrying it through to the end." [87] This is clearly not how Aldo has seemed to Jane. But it reinforces our sense that only a partial truth is likely to emerge from the stories of either Harry or Jane as they come to us through the scenario and the Capri letters. Once the pieces are put together, in fact, both Americans appear more than a bit ridiculous in their self-deception and obsessive pursuit of guilt. Harry never quite admits this, even though late in the novel he comes to understand both Jane and her need for Aldo. What he never does understand, but what the entire book has worked toward preparing us to comprehend, is his relationship with Dorotea. When Jane is killed in a plane crash, Harry marries Dorotea and returns with her to America; his final remarks to Mario reflect an anguished disappointment in Dorotea which Harry cannot fathom. The novel does not end so much as it turns us around to reconsider what we have learned. Harry has not known Dorotea; can we do any better?

Harry's every description of Dorotea stresses her sensuality and her vulgarity. Even Mario associates her with pagan rites and the sins of ancient Rome. As a peasant she seems to both sophisticated admirers an embodiment of the timeless magic Levi speaks of, a veritable Earth Mother. But as Mario notes, Harry enjoys thinking she comes from the *Ciociaria* when she is really from Apulia: "Romans always talk of the *Ciociaria* and its inhabitants with a certain contempt." [88] Much is made of Dorotea's cooking, especially her *scarcella:* "One could tell it was some patriarchal cake, sure indication of an ancient civilized tradition." Both men watch Dorotea bend with bare arms over the countertop and both men transform both cook and cooking into myth. Neither sees an Italian—potentially suburban American— housewife.

Soldati's final, triumphant irony appears as we come to recognize beneath the convoluted surface of *The Capri Letters* yet another instance of the emigrant's American myth. Harry and Jane make plausible—for a European, at least—an investigation of esoteric sexual pleasure and guilt and the further ecstasies of confession: Jane to Harry, and Harry to Mario. Soldati's sympathies lie, of course, with Italy; his strong, full-blooded peasant heroine emphasizes the nervous instability of his two expatriates. But there is the psychological motivation of the real woman to be accounted for if she is to be believably both more and less than Harry sees in her. Dorotea, the quiet base on which the novel rests, has dreamed from the start of Harry's taking her to America. She has understood Harry all along, he finally suspects, and has quietly endured his delusions because she "had a great plan, and this plan was so important, so vital to her that she tried at all costs to avoid any opposition to it from me. . . ." From the days of the liberation or before, "when as a child at home she had seen the emigrants leaving for America and heard of millionaires returning, she had dreamed of America as a paradise on earth. . . . From this came her unshakable sweetness to me, her compliance with each of my whims, her patience at all my rudeness and insults.

Superimposed on my figure she saw the Statue of Liberty, the entrance to New York." [89]

Harry finally marries Dorotea for a typically perverse reason: the idea of giving his two children a prostitute for their second mother is so abhorrent that "this suffering, with its possibilities of pleasure, . . . decided me to take the great step." [90] Dorotea has been careful not to shake his image of her, for "her love for America was mystical; and I was part of that love, its living symbol." [91] Unlike the symbolic loves of Harry and Jane, however, Dorotea's dream is attainable. She knows Harry delights in her promiscuity, so she lets him believe she sees other men. But she actually remains true to him, both because she is genuinely fond of him and because she is waiting for his curious impulses to carry them both off to America. It is almost a year after they do—in the final pages of the novel—that Harry begins to suspect how Dorotea has used him. America is every bit as wonderful as Dorotea had imagined. She delights Jane's parents, takes the children to her heart, and settles down in a little house on Long Island. She is happy; she tells Harry she is pregnant.

Harry is miserable. "The evil, Jane," he had said, "is never in others. It's always and only in ourselves who desire it." [92] It has become abundantly clear that Dorotea is not evil, and—clearer to us than to Harry—that she never was. Harry only knows that he no longer desires her. His dream of running away recalls once again the scattered references to his adolescence. He wants to "vanish into the world. Where to—the Far West, Mexico? No, no, I want to return to Rome." [93]

The Capri Letters could not exist without its two American characters and some such goal as America to motivate Dorotea. It is a superb novel, using the peculiar national illusions Soldati felt he could associate with Harry and Jane (other illusions might work as well) to explore an epistemological tangle worthy of Pirandello—it could never be mistaken for a treatise on aberrant sexuality. Soldati has been a lifelong admirer of Henry James, and the successful complexity of his novel is perhaps best seen as Jamesean. For it is not manipulation of narration alone that ensures its success but the fine sifting of the truth through a voice never fully in touch with reality and often wholly misled. "Then there we are," Strether can say. Harry cannot, and only the reader who sees beyond the book's three narrators will understand those six years as well as Dorotea does.

Green

There has been much less emigration from France than from Germany or Italy, and France has never openly chosen to "catch America" as the Soviets and Germans have. There has consequently been far less reliance on the simple imagery of immigration or American industrialism in serious French literature than in the other writing I have examined. I have ordered the discussions in the present chapter in what I take to be the ever-increasing complexity of the work examined. My examination of Julian Green thus occurs near the close of this book not to suggest that French art came late to the use of the American metaphor—quite the contrary is the case—but to emphasize the subtlety, complexity, and "modernity" of that use. Once we pass the local-color writing of Luc Durtain, Paul Morand, and André Maurois, who to the eye of one French critic at least had drawn America and Americans "as they are," [94] we come immediately to connotations of America which recall Kafka and Soldati.

Julian Green * was born and raised in France, and he writes in French. And yet his American parents and the few years he lived in America as student and refugee from the war provided him with an image of America that has proven useful in several of his books. Green's interest in sin and its effects has filled his novels and his journal with anguished discussions of sex—both as the chief temptation which challenges human sanctity and as an

---

* Julian Green has lived most of his life in France but retained his United States citizenship. Thus when he was recently elected to the French Academy to replace the late François Mauriac, he became its first non-French member. His journals, his essays on Samuel Johnson, the Brontës and Nathaniel Hawthorne, and all of his many novels but one are written in French. "I had a hard time learning English," Green has remarked, "so when I was about seven, mother read to me from the King James Bible."

emblem of all those trials which beset the psychological and spiritual life. The journal pages are filled with Green's own efforts to accommodate sexual desire to his sense of God's plan, and he often reminds himself that what God has created cannot be evil.[95] He persists in examining the entire spectrum of possibility, however, and repeatedly turns to America as a setting where the psychological effects of repression can be investigated. As with Soldati, the villain is usually labeled Puritanism. Green derives it historically from England; the link is implied in *Avarice House* and made explicit in the fragment, *The Distant Countries*. When Uncle Richard approaches his British cousin—in this last sketch—to invite her to Christmas dinner, she fears he means to attack her. By setting his two English women as exiles in the post-Civil War south, Green can challenge the Puritan he adapted from Hawthorne with the lush exoticism he always associated with Poe. Recalling the "enchanting whiteness" of her innocent youth in Kent, the daughter in *The Distant Countries* is troubled by the Deep South: she feels a stranger "in this country of obscurity and shadow where Nature untamed was still a menace to the habitations of man." She senses, beneath the thick undergrowth, a strange sweetness, a "world unknown," "of muffled, latent violence. . . ."[96]

Of the few writers examined in this book who actually experienced America directly, only Green took such explicit pains to treat his impressions from the first as raw materials for his art. His journal entries suggest he was never merely a traveler. He deliberately collected images which he thought might later prove useful, and he often did find a way to use them. Here are a few notes recalling a visit to the Deep South in 1934: "I walked under big oaks draped in moss with its long, restless fringes. Impossible to describe the effect of poverty and magnificence produced by this parasitic vegetation. There is something disturbing about the very quality of its luxuriance. Its color hesitates between pale gray and a dull greenish white; it is both theatrical and sinister, lending a haunting melancholy to Southern landscapes. Seen from a distance it reminds one of a head of hair." As he walked among the oaks he noted a "funereal chattering" from the treetops; "A vague, deep fear seized me suddenly and I ran away." He remarks

on another "interminable" avenue of oaks: "Always those same
long, torn curtains fluttering in the wind. Stout black branches
writhe like great snakes inside this gray horror. These trees often
give me such an unpleasant feeling that I am filled with a sort of
anguish, and yet they attract me, for they seem to give the most
beautiful picture imaginable of death." The trees on this occasion
remind him of old wizards watching over the south. "You feel
that by lingering in their shade, all things would become indif-
ferent and that death would be easy." [97]

"It seems to me," he continues, "that in the South, a barbarous
and menacing nature marches almost to the threshold of these
frail white-columned houses. It is all around us, with its buzzards
and its snakes and its nightmarish vegetation. And a melancholy
that seems to spring from the beginning of time." His visit to the
bizarre Cypress Swamp suggests a plunge "into an immemorial
past." The place reminds him again of death, and he thinks all
day of Poe's

> It was down by the dank tarn of Auber
> In the ghoul-haunted woodland of Weir.

The repeated references to Poe indicate the atmosphere Green is
trying to capture. But when he enters the disintegrating man-
sions, "splendid in a manner that seems peculiar to the Southern
states," and traces the shadows that move through "the low-ceil-
inged, silent rooms," [98] he is reminded more often of Hawthorne.
"It is all like a Hawthorne novel," he notes after a visit to Pringle
House in Charleston. "I should have liked to linger there awhile
and give myself up to idle fancies—the whole room emerging from
a swamp, the little, sharp-pointed head of a rat, with its long
moustaches, suddenly appearing above the surface of the stag-
nant water, just between the slender feet of the harpsi-
chord." [99]—Thus a Hawthorne transplanted from Puritan chill to
Gothic—or surreal—fever.

Both of these elements play their part in the lengthy fragment
Green included in his journal with the simple title, *The Distant
Countries* (1934). The powerful opening scene portrays Elizabeth
drawn into a voodoo ritual in the eerie, oppressive calm of the

forest evening. She has always been susceptible to the terror of the long veils of Spanish moss, "this growth like some species of light-colored hair, which hung down from the dark, gloomy branches," and which could be seen moving in some mysterious manner, "as though the breath of unseen mouths were stirring it." Green adds to the nightmare fright of his scene by using Hawthorne's favorite devices for suggesting the supernatural without literally invoking it. Elizabeth's guide "seemed to her" an incarnation of evil. "If the negroes were to be believed . . ." the powers of Satan lurked everywhere after nightfall. Elizabeth, however, does not believe the Negroes, does not imagine the darkness "filled with evil spirits of the African brand," for "she was English." [100] Thus the Poe-like atmosphere ultimately becomes no more than an ominous setting for the horror of Puritan repression which haunts the decaying southern estate of Elizabeth's hosts.

Green's first use of America, in *Avarice House* (1926), had employed this sexual terror almost exclusively, for the setting is the reinforcing sterility of "Ashley House." Here Emily Fletcher has grown to a kind of maturity—at least in her ability to hate and to emulate her mother's avarice—with no knowledge of sex or love whatever. She cannot understand the emotion playing about her minister in his congregation of possessive spinsters, and she is not prepared for the explosive force she unleashes when she tries to use a widower and his child to implement her own lust for possession. Green seems to have felt that we will accept his loveless family and its violent, repressed passions once we understand its American setting and the religious framework which leaves its perverse obsessions untouched.

The later, unfinished tale is more successful, for Green constructs a contest between his narrow Puritans and the natural world they regard as the enemy. In *The Distant Countries* Elizabeth recalls her Aunt Eveline's voice—a veritable conscience for the gay comfort of the plantation: "Its slightest whisper seemed to go all round the house . . . in search of some piece of naughtiness, some frivolous thought. You might be thinking you were alone, you might be humming a tune: and Aunt Eveline's voice . . . would then in some mysterious manner reach the ears of a lazy person who was not doing her lessons. . . ." This voice, adds the narrator, "was dreaded by Elizabeth no less than if it had been the voice of some dangerous person who might very well be carrying poison in the pocket of her apron." [101] How virulent this poison is, how lethal this suspicion of pleasure, this fear of sex, this repression of human passion can be is dissected with meticulous care in one of the fine novels of the twentieth century, *Moira* (1950).

Avarice House takes place in a Victorian ethos which underscores the suspicion of pleasure Green is portraying. By setting *Moira* in the University of Virginia in the 1920s, Green subjects his hero's hidebound fundamentalism to repeated challenge from a modern, secular world. The unknown threats from the primeval Georgia swamps have here been all but institutionalized in the love story of *Romeo and Juliet*—which Joseph (an effective copy of Aunt Eveline) flings to the floor in anger—and in the naked statues in the classical mode which force him to avert his eyes when entering or leaving the library.[102]

Moira is a novel of powerful intensity, and yet it could not succeed at all if we refused to grant Green his fantastic central figure. It is only in America, Green must have felt, that I can posit a village far off in the hills, a village where success in biblical quotation wins a young man social rank and scholarly fame. Here a boy can have a father, a blind father, who tells him that his body is his worst enemy, and who sends him off to the university prepared to fight the devil around every corner and across every page. Joseph's obsession with sin creates evil where none exists. He is paralyzed, incapable of sympathetic human relationship with anyone but a ministerial student—and even here he has no insight into the other's holiness and tries to dissuade him from what seems the fleshly capitulation of marriage. The suicide of a homosexual classmate he has refused to understand serves to highlight Joseph's central inability to live a human life, his failure to reconcile the conflicting currents of his own nature. For Green's preoccupation is basically psychological. He is interested in Joseph's fundamentalist sexual repression—his Americanness—only as a catalyst for the boy's emotional explosion. When Joseph does fall in love and his love is returned, he is totally unable to handle his emotions in a natural way. Love has always meant sin, so sin he must, with rage and violence. (Joseph's lovemaking closely resembles Fred's in Sartre's *The Respectful Prostitute.*) But the aftermath is also violent: Joseph kills the girl Moira.

Through his discovery of his own human frailty, Joseph is lifted free of his crippling religious heritage. The final pages of the book are notably unencumbered by biblical idiom. As he resists the temptation to escape and calmly accepts his punishment, Joseph is portrayed by Green as a fuller, healthier human being.

"I don't think anyone suspects what forms the substance of my sadness," Green recorded in his *Diary* for June 23, 1938. "I wanted to be a saint. That is all. . . ." Ten years later he notes: "I was thinking, a moment ago, that certain difficulties would not have existed in my life if I had not been subject to ungovernable fleshly appetites. My books would have been quite different. Better? I don't know, but different. My books are the books of a prisoner who dreams of freedom. . . . The novel I am writing is one long cry of anger against instinct. . . ." "Faith is the cause of this bitter conflict." [103] This particular investigation of the psychological fruits attending faith's encounter with instinct was *Moira.* In 1957 he returned once again to America as a suitable arena for his inquiries. "This morning," he writes, "I went back to my novel, which takes place in America (I hesitated a long time as to where the action should be situated). Not without melancholy do I remember America in 1920. I suffered a great deal there but finally became deeply attached to it. My holidays in Savannah came back to me. Those wide avenues were where the devil lay in wait for me with the poetry of night, the scent of night, and a setting of white columns and black shadows on the silvery streets, the mystery of squares filled with the odor of shrubs. I knew nothing, suspected nothing, but poison was already stealing into my heart—how, I don't know. At times, I thought of what one of the rue Cortambert nuns had said to me, all in white behind the grille of the little parlor that smelled of wax: 'Beware of the world . . . The world . . . The world's poison. . . .' All that is far away." [104]

But in *Each in His Darkness* (1960), none of this is really far away. Wilfred Ingram is a young man of twenty-four who fights and stumbles his way to sanctity. His holiness is not the marble goodness of Joseph with its flight from the human condition, however. It is the fruit of a faith that is sorely tried by the scented nights and black shadows of the world. The opening scenes suggest that Green had Joseph very much in mind when he worked out the character of his new central figure. When Wilfred visits the dilapidated southern mansion to attend Uncle Horace on his deathbed, we recall Joseph's dismay before the statuary at the college library. The first thing that meets Wilfred's eye is "a large and well-nigh naked woman of polished bronze. . . . She stood at the foot of the stairs smiling at the visitor and he, suitcase in hand, looked at her attentively." [105] The statue emerges as the central unifying symbol in a novel tight in structure and rich in implication. Wilfred's examination of the bronze woman is interrupted by a young mulatto serving girl—a girl he later thinks of as Uncle Horace's mistress. The statue also comes to suggest Alicia, a youthful passion of his old uncle. Finally, statue and Alicia alike blend in the person of Phoebe Knight, wife of Wilfred's cousin and the most difficult of all the tests which afflict Wilfred's religious faith.

The complex nature of that faith is perhaps best indicated by Wilfred's own reaction to the bronze lady. He not only returns her gaze attentively, but he also takes the first opportunity to continue his meditation: "Once more, he examined the bronze woman. To look at her roused evil thoughts, those of which you are bound to accuse yourself, but he had had so many since his last confession that one more would make no great difference. He was up to his eyes in mortal sin, and really the woman was beautiful. . . . She probably came from Europe where Uncle Horace . . . must have known women . . . exactly like this one. . . . Wilfred sighed. Uncle Horace was going to die, but he had had a good time. The young man looked a little longer at the perfect limbs, at all that flesh. To look meant a sort of happiness mingled with pain, with hunger, something that devastated the heart." A few moments later Wilfred is led past "a plaster frieze where mythological subjects could be identified. Dust outlined naked bodies with bold black strokes and Wilfred would have been very glad to examine the casts a little more fully, but he . . . could no more than glance right and left as he walked by." [106]

Wilfred has had a great many women, and he seems to want

most that he meets. But there is more than simple irony in the fact that everyone is attracted to what seems his goodness. His face radiates innocence, so much so that at one time or another most of the characters in the book notice it and remark on the purity of his faith. Wilfred does believe in his Catholicism, and his lust is a perpetual torment to him. He is, as someone who knows him well observes, "a pious rake." [107] He believes in sin and he believes that his body is the temple of the Holy Ghost. When he succumbs the aftermath is agony for him: "He opened his eyes and thought, 'Sunday.' The unbearable ordeal was about to begin. Between sin and repentance came an interval of disgust, a disgust of the flesh and still more horrible disgust of religion. What he was about to do would be done in spite of himself: leave his bed, deluge his body with cold water that would only purify his skin, dress like an automaton and pick up a Mass book with hands that still remembered the flesh they had caressed—all this nauseated him. . . . 'And what about me?' asked a voice in the innermost part of his being. . . . 'I love you.' " Wilfred doesn't answer the voice, but he does go off to Mass. At a later moment, "He threw himself at God, as one would let oneself drop from the top of a skyscraper." [108] Each time he sins he makes the painful struggle to regain his feet; this is what those who admire him mistake for childlike innocence.

But the ominous bronze statue and the dying Uncle Horace suggest a possible future fall too serious for recovery. Uncle Horace's life and his indulgence, particularly with Alicia, have brought him to the door of death apparently bereft of his faith. The association of the statue, Alicia, and Phoebe implies that if Wilfred succumbs to the adultery which offers the greatest temptation he has ever endured, Phoebe's goodness will be destroyed and he himself will be doomed to the terrors he sees in Uncle Horace. "Lord," Wilfred prays, "give me what I need to give faith to others. Make me believe."

"Why are you crying?" asked Uncle Horace. "Is it on my account?"

"On your account and on my account. For both of us."

Then whispering hoarsely, he said in a rush:

"Lord, give faith to both of us. Make it happen any way
You please, but give us faith. We're going to die."
    . . . He let a few seconds go by, then . . . murmured: "All's
well." [109]

Green manages his narrative so as to escape any mawkish
predictability. But as it turns out, these early prayers are all
answered. Uncle Horace apparently dies peacefully. Wilfred is
indeed—never without stressing the irony himself—the inspiration
for holiness in others. And the Lord does find a way to make it
happen that Wilfred will die with his faith intact. At the moment
his intimacy with Phoebe seems inevitable, Wilfred is more than
half led into a timely death, a death which the novel's final pages
directly insist leaves his body the very picture of beatitude.

The setting Green finally chose for this story contributes a great
deal to its dramatic and psychological credibility. "You Catholics
are the real Puritans of this country," Wilfred's cousin Angus
remarks. "If you were the majority, you would relax a little. And
at the same time you'd be less admirable and less tiresome." [110] As
an American Catholic, Wilfred can manifest the excruciating fear
of the flesh that Green called Puritanism. And he can be cast as an
exceptional case in a modern society which contains both the
agnostic homosexuality of Angus and the icy religiosity implied
in the sexless marriage of Phoebe and Mr. Knight. The kind of
sanctity Green is *not* interested in is caught neatly in Wilfred's
childhood recollection of the lady at the foot of the staircase: "An
opportune drapery concealed what should not be seen, back and
front." And still Wilfred had been warned, " 'Don't look.' " [111]
The way to God must be won wholly, by a total human being,
Green wants to say; his American setting brings him a fully
appointed battlefield. As it has done so frequently during his long
and productive career, America provides Green with a world
where sex can still mean sin and where sin is real enough to
precipitate the psychological dramas that make Green's novels.

Perse

I want to conclude this series of inquiries with a look at *Winds* (1945), a magnificent long poem by St.-John Perse, for it seems a logical step from the psychological landscapes of Soldati and Green to the cosmic terrain Perse makes of America. Paul Claudel was among the first to identify America as the dominant image in *Winds*. He calls Perse's lengthy epic a "spiritual adventure," a pursuit of "pure Space, the Sea beyond the sea!" Like Claudel himself, Perse directs his imaginative vision toward the west. "Is not the Setting Sun the homeland, the true homeland of all men of desire?" Claudel asks, "—that of the Maitreyea Buddha, toward which one day the fabulous Laotze set forth, and that which condemned Christopher Columbus to exile for his whole life?" [112] Columbus was Claudel's own metaphor for the seeker he recognized in Perse. In the music-drama *The Book of Christopher Columbus* (1930), Columbus is placed at the head of a lengthy series of travelers in Claudel's works who persistently set out to span the globe and draw together the entire universe. Columbus is not merely another *rassembleur de la terre,* however; he discovers new lands and carries the word of Christ—as his name suggests —to the farthest reaches of the globe.

But although Claudel praises Perse as a "successor to Columbus," [113] the author of *Winds* explores a private region beneath the historical conditioning of the soul; his search cannot really be identified with the social, public service Claudel associates with Columbus. Perse internalizes Claudel's quest. His exploration of self leads him to identify America, for so many Europeans an image of a physical *terra incognita,* with the unplumbed recesses of the subconscious, with—in the words of Archibald MacLeish—"the undiscovered and yet ancient continent." [114] "A novelist," Julian Green notes in *Diary,* "is like a scout commissioned to go and see what is happening in the depth of the soul." [115] These words could serve as epigraph for the sequence of poems by Perse which begins with *Exile* (1944) and culminates in the monumental *Winds*. Perse's poet is by vocation an exile who surrenders his home to wander in search of the primal truth the old civilizations have lost. In *Snow* (1944), Perse joins those who, he says, "each day, pitch camp further off from their birthplace, those who, each day, haul in their boat on other banks, know better, day by day, the course of illegible things; and tracing the rivers towards their source, between the green appearances they are caught up suddenly into that harsh glare . . ." [116] of prophetic, poetic utterance. Perse's Traveler feels the challenge of the wind from the west, a wind of violence which levels every wall, every law, every traditional barrier and signpost of his homeland. The wind promises freshness and renewal, so the poet, the Innovator, sets his course toward the west in *Winds* to seek out its source.

In his search for what is vital, for what lives "on the crests of the future as though on the clay slopes of the potter," [117] the poet journeys to the New World, whose "wolf-lore" [118] he associates with the New Year and the renewal of his tired European self. "Man is in question!" he cries, "and the eye's enlargement over the loftiest inner seas." [119] "Man is in question, and his integration. . . . My opinion is that we should live!" [120] He calls for new men and new ways. Most of the poet's quest for the source of the wind takes him across the American continent, both geographically and historically, but the future he finds there is not the machine civilization of Rilke and Céline. The renewal he sings is, rather, biblical. He is seeking, he says, a true scripture in the primeval schists of an ancient land: as in Goethe, America is here used to evoke what is old, what is fundamental, what has escaped the false choices of Europe.

This image of America recalls a passage from Green's journal: "I halted for a few moments in these dark [American] woods, in which there still lingers some vague aroma of prehistoric times. Surrounded as it is by that bare, unadorned landscape, this little fragment of the great primeval forest suggests a far distant recollection of childhood buried deep in the memory of someone who has now reached maturity. But generally speaking, apart from the few traces of the eighteenth century and of the War between the States, America is a vast blank page, while the country near Rome, to give no other example, is a sort of palimpsest." [121] Perse values this blank page, not as a sophisticate celebrating primitivistic innocence but as a seeker who would win elemental wisdom from primeval America for a world suffocating under the rubble of its decaying civilization.

Perse also associates America with vigorous, masculine action. Before crossing the plains to the Pacific, the poet pauses in the Deep South. He senses betrayal: "And of what have I been robbed there, in this sudden reversal of flowering camphor-trees —lingerie rumpled by every breath of wind? And the trade wind forsakes us, in the deserted drawing rooms, at the tulle whirlpools of the casements. . . ." The taste is "of black tuberose and mortuary chapel," and his ear catches the words " 'Great is my lassitude toward everything. . . .' We know the refrain," he adds. "It is the South." [122] These are new connotations to contrast with the fresh promise of continental America. The idleness, the rank vegetation, the oppressive climate all remind the poet of Death. He rejects the call of the South Wind and turns resolutely to the West.

As has been frequently noted, Perse is a poet of large concerns. He is a humanist who weighs man and his efforts in the light of all his hideous failures and yet finds much to praise and a future to trust. After the brief hesitance of *Eulogies* (1911), Perse's horses, ships, and birds, his Wanderer, Prince, and Poet follow persistently the westward, American course. (This movement and active assimilation helps distinguish Perse from the passive absorption of Whitman, whom he resembles in so many other ways.) Perse's *Winds* is one of his most challenging and ambitious poems. By using America as its central organizing image, he creates a metaphor capable of a suggestive richness and moving human significance it has rarely achieved in modern European literature.

I have encountered only one other metaphoric use of America which can match Perse's for inclusive scale. In "Americana," Giame Pintor casts America as the vision of the artist itself: "For after all what is a poetic revelation if not basically the discovery of a new world?" [123] Such an assertion carries us a long way from the social, political, and moral concerns of Mayakovsky and Brecht, but the distance simply emphasizes the wide range of connotation available to the artist who chooses to touch those strings in his audience tuned to respond to the word *America*.

Epilogue

It was a new heaven and a new earth.
—Henry James, "An Animated Conversation"

And yet, for all these unmistakable overtones of social or historic significance, it must not be thought that our writers necessarily use the image of the machine to direct attention to the historic fact of industrialization. To imply that would be to misconstrue their aims—to take the literary means for an end. As Emerson remarked, the artist "must" employ symbols in use in his day and nation, not in order to point in the direction of society, but rather to establish that interplay between art and experience that enables the great writer to "convey his enlarged sense to his fellow-men."
—Leo Marx, "Two Kingdoms of Force"

That Europe has had a deep and durable interest in the United States is the self-evident assumption with which this book began. This interest may at times have been tied to social, economic, or political events, but it rests ultimately on a human imperative which has little direct connection with the nation we call America; the need to imagine a place and a life somehow more perfect than—or at least different from—what we know at first hand easily

157

predates the voyages of Columbus. The artist seeking to comprehend his world and objectify his vision in a form calculated to stir
the recognition and touch the sympathy of his audience frequently turns to archetypal fantasies like this one—in the work
discussed here, America has often proved a helpful equivalent for
the limitless horizon of human aspiration. But as we well know,
the pain of an unfulfilled dream is not only poignant but bitter.
When Europe decided that America had it better, its double
disappointment was already assured. Life in Europe was not
significantly enriched once the Garden had been rediscovered,
and for those who came to feel that the United States was in fact
no Garden, the future which clearly followed the western course
of empire appeared more nightmare than dream. History and
human imagination thus combined to provide the artist with a
richly ambivalent metaphor, and while the range of accrued
connotation is broad, particular suggestions are readily con-
trolled.

"The myth about America which we cultivate in Europe," a
Dutch scholar once remarked, "has a psychological reality which
is much more important to us than the so-called truth about
America." [1] As I hope the survey in Part One has illustrated,
there has been a fundamental truth about Europe running deep
beneath these American fantasies, a truth reflecting "the stresses,
the conflicts . . . created in the European mind by the disintegration of the Europocentric world." [2] These tensions have required a basic reorientation of the European imagination, or—
to use Walter Kaufmann's helpful notion—they necessarily
prompted the creation of fresh "categories" of conceptualization.
It is in this capacity that the artist has always performed his most
significant social function. "The great artist is a creator of categories in terms of which posterity understands its own experiences, reinterprets the past, and fashions the future," Kaufmann
writes.

What makes a work of art a category is not the artist's
primary intent but posterity: what is decisive is that later
generations should come to understand their own experi-

ences in terms of the artist's creation. In this sense the love of *Romeo and Juliet* is a category, Faust is a category, Mephistopheles is a category, and the Bible is fuller of categories than any other book in all the world.[3]

Surely the invention of America established such a category, the stuff that dreams are made of. But where Kaufmann limits his remarks to the great artist, we must extend them to anyone who has ever used America to furnish the world he lives in—such, at any rate (to use Kaufmann's own test) would be the judgment of posterity. Generations without number have come to comprehend their own experience in terms of American imagery bequeathed them by earlier dreamers.

But it is of course true that the major artist bears a special relationship to the imagined worlds we live in. His genius may actually provide us with new ways to think about our experience: "He confers upon his readers a language whence he is able to derive a series of striking expressions which make it possible for them to think about what has been happening, and what is happening, in a way we could not have invented for ourselves." [4] But even this vision must build upon what we already are, what we already think—what and who we think we are. The artist most frequently shapes our future in terms we know from the present; he is often, to use Voznesensky's phrase, an "accoucheur of the new," fashioning today's language for what we wish to be into "categories" of freshly imaged possibility. The first four chapters of the present study describe the genesis and reach of one of history's major archetypal ideas. If the best of our modern artists had not recognized in this idea a valuable and flexible block to build with, we would have every cause for surprise. But as I illustrate through the selective discussions of my final chapter, an impressive succession of European writers have both demonstrated and enhanced the rich suggestions of the American idea. I have done little more than sample the uses they have found for these connotations of America. But by limiting the number of artists and works examined, I hope I have suggested some of the ways one cluster of images has been made to transcend its immediate referrent to achieve the universality of Kaufmann's "categories."

As I remarked earlier, it would be reductive to think of complex literary works simply as they use the American (or any other) metaphor. But some generalization is possible, and it may clarify the development I sought in the previous discussion. Thus, in Mayakovsky's work, for example, America can be made to suggest both the decadent past and the technocratic future; it serves to articulate a confrontation through which Ivan claims that future. In later poems Mayakovsky's America can shift to represent the years ahead as both fruitful and sterile. Kafka, Céline, and Pavese borrow the imagery of immigration to isolate their European characters, but then invoke America to embody their comment on the future of civilization itself. When Brecht turned from the portrayal of human selfishness and greed to indictment of the capitalism he felt nourished it, his America was transformed from a simple neutral setting to one of his central symbols for modern rapacity. For Soldati and Green, Americans could be fitted with an intensely self-conscious sexuality, a capacity for guilt enormously useful to the psychological novelist. And finally, in Perse, the myth of the New World has been made to subsume the primeval roots of us all, the still legible beginning to which, not simply the individual immigrant, but civilization itself must return for its necessary fresh start.

Such a list is obviously inadequate, both with regard to the works themselves and to my examination of them. But it does serve to illustrate my reason for placing the discussions of the last chapter in their present order. I have wanted to indicate a movement from the simple to the more complex, not only in the connotations attached to America but also in its fictive uses and—perhaps the two come to the same thing—in the nature of the total work under study. Such an organizational principle is a loose one; I have relied on it simply to avoid others that were further from my purpose, and I do not mean to insist upon it. But there does seem a considerable distance from the naïve metaphors of the Soviets and the often simplistic works they serve to the rich connotations America provides for the intricate art of the Italian and French authors mentioned here. There are undoubtedly ample reasons for the contrast I note, some reflecting the extent of actual knowledge of America through immigration or other communication, others touching literary heritage, native sensibility, audience expectation, and general creative climate. But whatever the causes, I find the works examined in the later pages of this book the most inventive and challenging—both absolutely and in terms of my present investigation.

Quite apart from the intrinsic interest of the writing examined, however, the functioning of a major image cluster has seemed to me a fascinating indication of how artists employ the material their culture makes available to them. Modern European writers have found wide and varied use for their American metaphor. In my initial review of Europe's creation of an American image I remarked that the growth of that image, the development of its connotations, may well have ceased, that the metaphoric suggestiveness of America may have become virtually fixed. But whether or not such a hypothesis will prove valid, I do not anticipate less frequent use of America in European literature. There is far too much it can help a writer to do and to say.

Notes

Chapter I

1. Edmundo O'Gorman, *The Invention of America: An Inquiry into the Historical Nature of the New World and the Meaning of Its History* (Indiana University Press, 1961). This extraordinary book has been of inestimable value to me. I have relied on it heavily during the first pages of this essay but have greatly simplified O'Gorman's complex and thoroughly documented argument.

2. O'Gorman, Plate X.

3. O'Gorman, pp. 137, 139. For a fuller discussion of the slight imaginative impact of the explorations, see G. V. Scammell, "The New Worlds and Europe in the Sixteenth Century," *The Historical Journal*, 12 (1969), 389-412.

4. For a discussion of Europe's unnoticed transfer of assumptions from the Spanish south to the British north, see Harold Jantz, "The Myth about America: Origins and Extensions," *Jahrbuch für Amerikastudien*, 7 (1962), 7-8.

5. Carl Wittke, "The American Theme in Continental European Literatures," *The Mississippi Valley Historical Review*, 28 (June 1941), 3.

Chapter II

1. See George Sanderlin, *Across the Ocean Sea* (New York: Harper & Row, 1966). The stories are told more fully there in the Introduction and in Chapter I; these and several other fables are recounted in Howard Mumford Jones, *O Strange New World* (New York: The Viking Press, 1964), Chapters I-II; cf. Robert R.

Cawley, *Unpathed Waters* (New York: Octagon Books, 1967), pp. 1-70; and Harry Levin, *The Myth of the Golden Age in the Renaissance* (Bloomington & London: Indiana University Press, 1969). Within a rough outline of North America on a map printed in 1701 appears the remark, "This Continent with the adjoining Islands is generally supposed to have been Anciently unknown, though there are not wanting some, who will have even the Continent its self to be no other, than the Insula ATLANTIS of the Ancients." The map is the first in Edward Wells, *A Treatise of Antient and Present Geography together with a Set of Maps, Design'd for the Use of Young Students in the Universities;* it appears as the first flyleaf of *The Oxford Atlas* (Oxford University Press, 1951).

2. For an interesting account of Europe's shifting conception of non-European lands and people, see Henri Baudet, *Paradise on Earth,* trans. Elizabeth Wentholt (New Haven: Yale University Press, 1965); for a useful summary of the part played by Adam and the Garden in recent American criticism, see Frederick I. Carpenter, " 'The American Myth': Paradise (To Be) Regained," *Publications of the Modern Language Association,* 74 (December 1959), 599-606. For Europe's concept of America as a garden see Henry Nash Smith's influential book, *Virgin Land.*

3. Any study of primitivism must begin with the work of Gilbert Chinard, especially *L'Exotisme Américain dans la Littérature Française au XVIe Siècle* (Paris: Hachette, 1911) and *L'Amérique et le Rêve Exotique dans la Littérature Française au XVIIe et au XVIIIe Siècle* (Paris: Hachette, 1913); for a full checklist of Chinard's writing, including his Chateaubriand essays, see *The Princeton University Library Chronicle* (Spring 1965). See also A. O. Lovejoy and George Boas, *Primitivism and Related Ideas in Antiquity* (Baltimore: Johns Hopkins Press, 1935), and Baudet, op cit.

4. O'Gorman speaks of the "apocalyptic impatience" felt by missionaries to whom the end of the world seemed near; cf. Marcel Bataillon, "Nouveau monde et fin du monde," *L'Education Nationale,* 32 (December 11, 1952), 3-6.

5. See Henry S. Bausum's discussion and extension of Jones, op. cit.: "Edenic Images of the Western World: A Reappraisal," *The South Atlantic Quarterly,* 67 (Autumn 1968), 672-687.

6. Gilbert Chinard, "The American Dream," *Literary History of the United States,* ed. Robert Spiller, et al. (New York: Macmillan, 1959), p. 193.

7. *The Complete Works of Montaigne,* trans. Donald M. Frame (Stanford: Stanford University Press, 1958), p. 150.

8. Ibid., p. 152.

9. Ibid., p. 153.

10. Ibid., p. 154.

11. Ibid., p. 158. For a discussion of Renaissance portraits of Indians on classical models, see Jones, pp. 28-32.

12. *Montaigne,* p. 693.

13. For valuable first steps toward a history of the idea that civilization moves westward, see Harold Jantz, "The Myths about America: Origins and Extensions," *Jahrbuch für Amerikastudien,* 7 (1962), 10-14. Several nineteenth-century observers decided that the future belonged to America and Russia; for an example, see *Literary History of the United States,* pp. 206-207.

14. *Montaigne,* p. 695. Long before Americans were condemned for their acquisitiveness, America was seen as encouraging greed in Europeans; see, e.g., Harold von Hofe, "The Halberstadt Poets and the New World," *The Germanic Review,* 32 (December 1957), 243-254.

15. For a discussion of this play and other Shakespearean references to America, see Sidney Lee, *Elizabethan and Other Essays,* ed. F. S. Boas (Oxford: The Clarendon Press, 1929), pp. 291 ff.; cf. A. L. Rowse, *The Elizabethans and America* (New York: Harper & Brothers), pp. 197-200, and Leo Marx, "Shakespeare's American Fable," *The Machine in the Garden* (New York: Oxford University Press, 1964).

16. The passage is adapted from More's *Utopia.* Cf. Rowse, p. 193.

17. See *The Faerie Queene,* Book IV, xi, 22 and Book II, "Proem," i-iv. For relevant discussion and full bibliographic reference, see Roy Harvey Pearce, "Primitivistic Ideas in the Faerie Queene," *The Journal of English and Germanic Philology,* 44 (April 1945), 139-151. More than a century later Jonathan Swift located one of *his* fairylands, Brobdingnag, close to the coast of North America.

18. See Jones, p. 37.

19. Robert B. Heilman, *America in English Fiction, 1760-1800* (Baton Rouge: Louisiana State University Press, 1937), pp. 25-26. Cf. Robert R. Cawley, *The Influence of the Voyagers in Non-Dramatic English Literature Between 1550 and 1650. . . .* (unpublished dissertation, Harvard, 1921), and, by the same author, *Unpathed Waters: Studies in the Influence of the Voyagers on Elizabethan Literature* (New York: Octagon Books, 1967).

20. For two well-documented discussions, see John C. Lapp, "The New World in French Poetry of the Sixteenth Century," *Studies in Philology*, 45 (1948), 151-164, and Dorothy Dondore, *The Prairie and the Making of Middle America* (Cedar Rapids, Iowa: The Torch Press, 1926), pp. 84 ff.

21. The conclusions are those of Beulah H. Swigard, who examined some 646 articles and 36,000 pages of the *Encyclopédie;* see *The Americas as Revealed in the Encyclopédie* (unpublished dissertation, Urbana, Ill., 1939).

22. Antoine-François Prevost draws on this tradition when the hero of *Manon Lescaut* (1731) plans to flee New Orleans and "seek death among savages or in the claws of wild beasts." Earlier in the novel, America serves to suggest the terrors of exile to the unknown; Prevost brightens the image as the hopes of his lovers rise: "The further we advanced toward America, the more I felt my heart expand and grow tranquil." *Manon Lescaut,* trans. Donald M. Frame (New York: New American Library, 1961), pp. 185, 175; cf. 172, 179, 180. See also Benjamin Bissell, *The American Indian in English Literature of the Eighteenth Century* (New Haven: Yale University Press, 1925), and Roy Harvey Pearce, *The Savages of America: A Study of the Indian and the Idea of Civilization* (Baltimore: Johns Hopkins Press, 1953).

23. Emma Kate Armstrong, "Chateaubriand's America," *Publications of the Modern Language Association of America*, 22 (1907), 370.

24. Raymond Lebègue, "Reflexions sur Chateaubriand," *Cahiers du Sud,* No. 357 (Septembre-Octobre 1960), 182.

25. Quoted in Lida von Krokow, "American Characters in German Novels," *The Atlantic Monthly,* 68 (1891), 832. For Cooper's reputation abroad, see *Literary History of the United States,*

p. 624, and Preston A. Barba, "Cooper in Germany," *German American Annals,* 12 n.e. (January-February 1914), 3-60.

26. Cf. Virgil L. Jones, "Gustave Aimard," *Southwest Review,* 15 (1929-30), 452-468.

27. See Klaus Mann, "Karl May, Hitler's Literary Mentor," *The Kenyon Review,* 2 (Autumn 1940), 391-400; Mann is quoted in Wittke, p. 16. See also "The American West of Karl May," *American Quarterly,* 19 (Summer 1967), 249-258.

28. See Sigmund Skard, *The American Myth and the European Mind: American Studies in Europe 1776-1960* (Philadelphia: University of Pennsylvania Press, 1961), p. 17.

29. Cf. *Literary History of the United States,* pp. 197, 198 ff. (The verse lines are Byron's.) For a thorough discussion, see Durand Echeverria, *Mirage in the West: A History of the French Image of American Society to 1815* (Princeton: Princeton University Press, 1957); Kenneth N. McKee, "The Popularity of the 'American' on the French Stage during the Revolution," *Proceedings of the American Philosophical Society,* 83 (September 1940), 479-491; and Gilbert Malcolm Fess, *The American Revolution in Creative French Literature (1775-1937)* (Columbia: University of Missouri Press, 1941). For further introduction to the subject in other countries, see Valentin Kiparsky, *English and American Characters in Russian Fiction* (Berlin: Saladruck Steinkopf & Sohn, 1964); F. M. Bicknell, "Yankee in British Fiction," *Outlook,* No. 96 (1910), 632-639; Robert B. Heilman, *America in English Fiction 1760-1800* (Baton Rouge: Louisiana State University Press, 1937); Myron F. Brightfield, "America and the Americans, 1840-1860, as Depicted in English Novels of the Period," *American Literature* (November 1959), 309-324; Douglas M. Schwegal, *The Use of American Motifs by British Poets of the Romantic Period* (unpublished dissertation, Minnesota 1960; *DA* 31, p. 1952); Charles E. Shain, *A British Image of America and the Americans as They Appeared in the English Novel 1830-1890* (unpublished dissertation, Princeton, 1955; *DA* 15, p. 830); Nils Erik Enkvist, "Caricatures of Americans on the English Stage Prior to 1870," *Commentationes Humanarum Litterarum,* 18 (Helsingfors: Societas Scientiarum Fennica), 1-168; Frederick S. Boas, "American Scenes, Tudor to Georgian, in the

English Literary Mirror," *The English Association Presidential Address* (London: Oxford University Press, 1944); Donald Heiney, *America in Modern Italian Literature* (New Brunswick, N.J.: Rutgers University Press, 1964), Part I; Paul C. Weber, *America in Imaginative German Literature in the First Half of the Nineteenth Century* (New York: Columbia University Press, 1926), pp. 33-41; Dorothy Anne Dondore, *The Prairie and the Making of Middle America: Four Centuries of Description* (Cedar Rapids, Iowa: The Torch Press, 1926), pp. 270-283, 300-305; Hjalmar Hjorth Boyesen, "America in European Literature," *Literary and Social Silhouettes* (New York: Harper & Brothers, 1887, 1894), pp. 117-130; Carl Wittke, "The American Theme in Continental European Literatures," *The Mississippi Valley Historical Review,* 28·(June 1941), 3-26. For two thorough surveys of America in German literature, see Gerhard Desczyk, "Amerika in der Phantasie Deutscher Dichter," *Jahrbuch der Deutsch-Amerikanischen Historischen Gesellschaft von Illinois,* 24 (1924), 7-142, and Harold Jantz, "Amerika im Deutsches Dichten und Denken," *Deutsche Philologie im Aufriss,* ed. Wolfgang Stammler, Band III (Berlin: Erich Schmidt Verlag, 1962), 309-372.

30. The most thorough study of the Revolution's literary impact is Henry Safford King, "Echoes of the American Revolution in German Literature," *University of California Publications in Modern Philology,* 14 (June 24, 1929), i-vii, 23-193, but see two well-known earlier essays, J. T. Hatfield and E. Hochbaum, "The Influence of the American Revolution upon German Literature," *Americana Germanica,* 3 (1899-1900), 338-385, and John A. Walz, "The American Revolution and German Literature," *Modern Language Notes,* 16 (1901), 168-176, 206-209, 225-231. See also Harold von Hofe, "The Halberstadt Poets and the New World," *Germanic Review,* 32 (1957), 243-254. For an exhaustive background investigation, see Eugene Edgar Doll, "American History as Interpreted by German Historians from 1770 to 1815," *Transactions of the American Philosophical Society,* 38 n.s. (June 1949), 421-534.

31. See Weber, pp. 2, 3-4, 268, and Lydia Elizabeth Wagner, "The Reserved Attitude of the Early German Romanticists toward America," *German Quarterly,* 16-17 (1943-44), 8-12.

32. Weber, p. 269. For the persistent influence of Cooper and

Chateaubriand discussed earlier, see Lida von Krockow, "American Characters in German Novels," *The Atlantic Monthly*, 68 (1891), 832-833.

33. Weber, pp. 270 f.

34. Goethe, "Stoff und Gehalt," *Gedenkausgabe der Werke, Briefe und Gespräche*, 14 (Zurich: Artemis-Verlag, 1949), 378-382. See also Anna Hellersberg-Wendriner, "America in the World View of the Aged Goethe," *Germanic Review*, 14 (1939), 275, and Friedrich C. Sell, "American influences upon Goethe," *The American-German Review*, 9 (April 1943), 17. Goethe's enthusiasm for America as an image of the future came to exercise an important influence on Thomas Mann. During his Wagnerian, individualist phase, Mann associated Americanism with the inhumanity of industrial automation and mass education. But Wagner gave way to the mature Goethe as Mann's model. Sometime before the Second World War, with his Germany disintegrating around him, Mann became more socially and politically aware than he had ever been before. Like Goethe, he came to see in America's "streamline" (his word) culture a hopeful type for the future: "There is something of a grandiose matter-of-factness in this [Goethe's] enthusiasm for world-wide technological rationality, a feeling that the ailing world had to be disenchanted and disencumbered from sentimental memories that impeded life and obstructed progress." Trans. Agnes E. Meyer. Quoted in Heinz Politzer, "America in the Later Writings of Thomas Mann," *Modern Language Forum*, 37 (September-December 1952), 93; see also Erich A. Frey, *Amerika in Dem Werken Thomas Manns* (unpublished dissertation, Southern California, 1964). Mann emigrated to America in 1938, and he conceived, for the final two volumes of *Joseph und Seine Brüder* (1938, 1945), an Egypt remarkably American. He makes use, not only of the bright California sky, but of FDR and the New Deal as well—and the story of Joseph develops more than a little along the lines of the immigrant tale.

35. Preston A. Barba, "Emigration to America Reflected in German Fiction," *German American Annals*, 16 o.s. (1914), 194. For another discussion of immigrant literature, see Carl Wittke, "The America Theme in Continental European Literature," *The Mississippi Valley Historical Review*, 27 (1941-42), especially pp. 7-18.

36. I take these later figures from Lawrence Marsden Price, *The Reception of United States Literature in Germany* (Chapel Hill: University of North Carolina Press, 1966), p. 35.

37. Weber, pp. 271-272; cf. George H. R. O'Donnell, "Gerstäcker in America, 1837-1843," *Publications of the Modern Language Association*, 42 (1927), 1036-1043, A. J. Prahl, "America in the Works of Gerstäcker," *Modern Language Quarterly*, 4 (March-December 1943), 213-224, Nelson Van de Luyster, "Gerstäcker's Novels about Emigrants to America," *American-German Review*, 20 (June-July 1954), 22-23, 36, and Alfred Kolb, "Gerstäcker's America," *Thoth* (Winter 1966), 12-21.

38. Weber, p. 272; cf. William Paul Dallmann, *The Spirit of America as Interpreted in the Works of Charles Sealsfield* (unpublished dissertation, Washington University, St. Louis, 1935). For a full discussion of the subject, see Preston A. Barba, "Emigration to America Reflected in German Fiction," *German American Annals*, 12 n.s. (November-December 1914), 193-227. For a Scots novelist with similar aims, see Charles E. Shain, "John Galt's America," *American Quarterly*, 8 (Fall 1956), 254-263.

39. John N. Morris, "Milton and the Imagination of Time," *The South Atlantic Quarterly*, 67 (Autumn 1968), 654. Morris attributes this comment to Marjorie Nicolson.

40. See G. D. Lillibridge, "The American Impact Abroad, Past and Present," *The American Scholar*, 35 (Winter 1965-66), 43-44. For a model study of early British promotion literature, see Howard Mumford Jones, "The Colonial Impulse," *Proceedings of the American Philosophical Society*, 90 (May 1946), 131-161; for a well-documented examination of later promotional literature and immigrant expectations, see Merle Curti and Kendall Birr, "The Immigrant Image in Europe, 1860-1914," *The Mississippi Valley Historical Review*, 37 (September 1950), 203-230. For a description of the Statue of Liberty in Laboulaye's own words, see his letter to Mary Booth, *The French American Review*, 2 (1949), 235-236. Laboulaye was a persistent and articulate proponent of the idea that America represented the future: his utopian fantasy, *Paris in America* went through 27 editions (printings?) by 1872.

41. Cf. Gilbert Chinard, "Eighteenth Century Theories on

America as a Human Habitat," *Proceedings of the American Philosophical Society,* 91 (February 1947), 27. For a thorough study of French immigration, see Howard Mumford Jones, *America and French Culture, 1750-1848* (Chapel Hill: University of North Carolina Press, 1927), especially chapters IV-V. The story of the immigrants who decided not to stay for one reason or another and eventually returned home is difficult to trace and will perhaps never be known; for an introductory note, see Alfred Vagts, "The Ebb-Tide of Immigration: Germans Returning from America," *American-German Review,* 21 (October-November 1954), 30-33.

42. See "Search for Eden, an Eighteenth-Century Disaster: Memoires of Count de Lezay-Marnesia," Sylvia Harris, trans., *The Franco-American Review,* 2 (Summer 1937), 50.

43. *Literary History of the United States,* p. 215; cf. Michael Kraus, "America and the Utopian Ideal in the Eighteenth Century," *The Mississippi Valley Historical Review,* 22 (March 1936), 487-504.

44. See Janina W. Hoskins, "The Image of America in Accounts of Polish Travelers of the 18th and 19th Centuries," *The Quarterly Journal of the Library of Congress,* 22 (July 1965), 240. The essay concludes that the accounts studied agree in regarding America as the "land of freedom"; see p. 243.

45. See James F. Marshall, "Stendhal and America," *The French American Review,* 2 (1949), 242. Marshall suggests the threat of emigration might have been an effort by Stendhal to blackmail his family—yet another use for America; see pp. 241-242.

46. Harold von Hofe, "The Halberstadt Poets and the New World," *The Germanic Review,* 32 (December 1957), 253.

47. See Jantz, "The Myth about America," p. 15, and Ruth Berges, "Lenau's Quest in America," *The American-German Review,* 28 (April-May 1962), 14-17.

48. For an interesting effort to trace the growth of American industrialism and its impact on Europe, see Merle Curti, "America at the World Fairs, 1851-1893," *The American Historical Review,* 55 (1949-50), 833-856. Another persistent enemy of America was Baudelaire, who equated the United States with bourgeois France and the persecution of Poe with his own. As Lawrence was to do, Baudelaire focused many of his reservations

in a conception of Benjamin Franklin. See James S. Patty, "Baudelaire's View of America," *Kentucky Romance Quarterly,* 2 (1955), especially p. 171.

49. Howard C. Rice, "Seeing Ourselves as the French See Us," *The French Review,* 21 (1947-48), 440-441, and Jean-Paul Sartre, "American Novelists in French Eyes," *The Atlantic Monthly,* 178 (July-December 1946), 114.

50. Simon Jeune, *De F. T. Graindorge à A. O. Barnabooth: Les Types Américains dans le Roman et le Théâtre Français (1861-1917),* (Paris: Didier, 1963), p. 459.

51. André Bellessort, "L'Américanisme en France," *La Revue Hebdomadaire* (21 Avril 1928), 265. See also Kornel Huvos, *Cinq Mirages Américains: Les Etats-Unis dans l'oeuvre de Georges Duhamel, Jules Romains, André Maurois, Jacques Maritain et Simone de Beauvoir* (Paris: Didier, 1972); for bibliography, see pp. 349-363.

52. I draw here on a manuscript text by James C. Cowan which Professor Cowan generously placed at my disposal. It has since appeared as *D. H. Lawrence's American Journey* (Cleveland/London: The Press of Case Western Reserve University, 1970).

53. In his discussion of the *Studies,* David Cavitch illustrates the important part the American myth might play in a man's life. Lawrence's essays, Cavitch notes, "create a symbolic global geography, establishing America as the point of inevitable crisis in the next development of consciousness. He invested the locality with much of his deepest intuition about the self, particularly about himself. In doing so, he made his imagination dependent, to a large degree, upon the continuing inspiration of the American continent. He strove thereafter to realize consciously the meaning of the place that he had encoded with personal significance. The attitude toward America which he carried forward from these studies for several years and through many works is, understandably enough, proprietary, hierophantic, and illusional. In a very intimate sense, it is his country. . . . The extremes of anticipation and of aversion which mark his long-deliberated approach to the United States indicate how much of his inner life . . . he had invested in the image of America." *D. H. Lawrence and the New World* (New York: Oxford University Press, 1969), pp. 100, 103.

54. Cf. Melvin J. Lasky, "America and Europe: Trans-
atlantic Images," and Marcus Cunliffe, "European Images of
America," in *Paths of American Thought,* Arthur M. Schlesinger, Jr.
and Morton White, eds. (Boston: Houghton Mifflin Com-
pany, 1963), pp. 465-491, 492-514. Cf. Shigeto Tsuru, "Japanese
Images of America," ibid., pp. 515-530; A. N. J. den Hollander,
"The Dutch Image of America," *Delta,* 2 (September 1959),
36-45; Elsa Gress Wright, "Almost in the Family" [America in
Scandinavian Literature], *Kenyon Review,* 24 (1962), 282-303; and
E. E. Larsen, "Swedish Commentators on America, 1638-1865,"
Bulletin of the New York Public Library, 67 (1963), 349-359. For a
useful effort to separate this myth from the images fostered by
translations of American literature, see Harry Levin, "France-
Amérique: The Transatlantic Refraction," *Refractions* (New
York: Oxford University Press, 1966), pp. 212-220.

Chapter III

1. *Literary History of the United States,* p. 215. This sentence sums
up and concludes Gilbert Chinard's essay. See also Sigmund
Skard, "The Image of America in Europe," in *American Civilization: An Introduction,* ed. A.N.J. den Hollander and Sigmund Skard
for the European Association for American Studies (London:
Longman Group, Ltd., 1968), pp. 455-473; Skard's extensive
bibliography appears on pp. 502-508.

2. For a discussion of this exaltation, see Jean Babelon, "Dé-
couverte du Monde et Littérature," *Comparative Literature,* 2
(Spring 1950), 157-166.

3. Quoted as epigraph to Cyrille Arnavon, *L'Américanisme et
Nous* (Paris: Editions Mondiales, 1958). The central figure of
Huysmann's *Against the Grain* (1884) blames the vulgarity and
mediocrity of contemporary life on American influence. The
same complaint can be found in André Bellessort, "L'Américanisme en France," *La Revue Hebdomadaire* (21 Avril 1928), 259-277.
For a discussion of more recent attitudes, see Kornel Huvos,"Vers
un renouveau du 'mirage américain' dans les lettres françaises,"
The French Review, XLVII (December, 1973), 291-301.

4. John Stuart Mill, "M. de Tocqueville on *Democracy in America,*" *The Philosophy of John Stuart Mill,* ed. Marshall Cohen (New York: Modern Library, 1961), p. 172.

5. From an unsigned article in the London Times Literary Supplement (1954); reprinted in Kay S. House, ed., *Reality and Myth in American Literature* (Greenwich, Conn.: A Fawcett Premier Book, 1966), p. 285.

6. Cyrille Arnavon, *L'Américanisme et Nous,* p. 9.

7. Leslie Fiedler, "Italian Pilgrimage: The Discovery of America," *The Kenyon Review,* 14 (Summer 1952), 377.

Chapter IV

1. Eugène Vinaver, "Introduction," *Malory: Works* (New York: Oxford University Press, 1954), p. ix.

2. *The Tales of Chekhov,* trans. Constance Garnett, 12 (New York: Macmillan, 1922), pp. 122, 123. Elsa Gress Wright's description of a nineteenth-century Danish children's book, *The Flight to America,* bears a remarkable resemblance to Chekhov's story. See *The Kenyon Review,* 24 (1962), 287.

3. The translation is by Alfred Kolb. Cf. "Gerstäcker's America," *Thoth,* 7 (Winter 1966), 13.

4. Honoré Balzac, *Old Goriot,* trans. Marion A. Crawford (Penguin Classics, 1951), p. 131.

5. Mihail Lermontov, *A Hero of Our Time,* trans. Martin Parker (New York: Collier Books, 1962), p. 54.

6. See Jean Simon, "L'Amérique Telle Que l'Ont Vue les Romanciers Française (1917-1937)," *Etudes Anglaises,* 1 (1937), 501. Georges Lemaître complains that when Giraudoux carries his hero to the United States, "he refrains from giving the slightest suggestion of American local colour." *Four French Novelists* (New York: Oxford University Press, 1938), p. 290.

7. Fyodor Dostoevsky, *The Brothers Karamazov,* trans. David Magarshack (Baltimore: Penguin Books, 1963), pp. 898-99.

8. *Atlantis,* trans. Adele and Thomas Seltzer (London: T. Werner Laurie Ltd., n.d.), p. 10.

9. Ibid., p. 20.

10. Ibid., p. 48.

11. Ibid., p. 113.

12. Ibid., p. 319.

13. Ibid., p. 347.

14. *Job, the Story of a Simple Man,* trans. Dorothy Thompson (New York: Grosset & Dunlap, 1931), p. 3.

15. *The Maurizius Case,* trans. Caroline Newton (New York: Liveright, 1929), p. 313.

16. Ibid., p. 333.

17. Ibid., p. 334.

18. Ibid., p. 335.

19. Ibid., p. 344.

20. Ibid., p. 346. Cf. the discussion of Cesare Pavase's *The Moon and the Bonfire* below.

21. Ibid., pp. 350-351.

22. Quoted in Carlo Levi, "Italy's Myth of America," *Life,* 23 (July 7, 1947), 85.

23. "America and Italy: Myths and Realities," *Italian Quarterly,* 3 (Spring 1959), 3.

24. Ignazio Silone, *Fontamara* (Milan: Mondadari, 1962), p. 42. Trans. Donald Heiney, *America in Modern Italian Literature* (New Brunswick, N.J.: Rutgers University Press, 1964), p. 118. Mr. Heiney's book contains full discussions of Moravia and Silone; it is a valuable introduction to the present subject. For another treatment, see Leslie A. Fiedler, "Italian Pilgrimage: The Discovery of America," *The Kenyon Review,* 14 (Summer 1952), 359-377.

25. *Christ Stopped at Eboli: The Story of a Year,* trans. Frances Frenaye (New York: Farrar, Straus and Company, 1947), pp. 45-46.

26. Ibid., pp. 46-47.

27. Ibid., p. 122.

28. Ibid., p. 123.

29. Ibid., p. 96.

30. "The Boy," trans. Peter B. Warren in *Modern Italian Short Stories,* ed. Marc Slonim (New York: Simon and Schuster, 1954), pp. 102, 103.

31. *Eboli,* p. 186.

32. *Rosa,* trans. Carla Barford and Sheila Hodges (London: Eyre & Spottiswoode, 1963), p. 56.

33. Ibid., p. 104.

34. Ibid., p. 95.

35. Quoted in Carlo Levi, *Life,* 23 (July 7, 1947), 89.

36. Vladimir G. Korolenko, *In a Strange Land,* trans. Gregory Zilboorg (New York: Bernard G. Richards Co., 1925), p. 1. For a similar use of America to highlight Russian innocence, see Fyodor Dostoevsky, *The Possessed,* 1, Part 4, Chapter 4.

37. "Aunt Bess, In Memoriam," trans. Ben Johnson in *Modern Italian Short Stories,* ed. Marc Slonim (New York: Simon and Schuster, 1954), p. 327.

38. Ibid., pp. 326-327.

39. Ibid., pp. 327-328.

40. Ibid., p. 341.

41. See Ernest Poole, "Maxim Gorki in New York," *The Slavonic and East European Review,* 22 (May 1944), 81, and Mark Twain, "The Gorki Incident," ibid. (August 1944), 37-38.

42. Quoted by Herman Bernstein in his preface to Andreyev, *Satan's Diary* (New York: Boni & Liveright, 1920), p. xii.

43. *Letters of Gorky and Andreyev, 1899-1912,* Peter Yershov, ed., Lydia Weston, trans., (New York: Columbia University Press, 1958), p. 85.

44. Maxim Gorky, *Articles and Pamphlets* (Moscow: Foreign Languages Publishing House, 1951), p. 85.

45. Ibid., p. 9. Gorky's method here should be contrasted with his attack on the film in "O kinematografe" (1909).

46. Ibid., p. 88.

47. Andreyev died in exile, planning the trip to America which had so often occupied his thoughts. "When I was a child I loved America," he told Herman Bernstein in 1908. "Perhaps Cooper and Mayne Reid, my favorite authors in my childhood days, were responsible for this. I was always planning to run away to America." While yet a boy Andreyev did set out for America; he got only from Orel to Petrograd, not a great deal farther than the boys in Chekhov's story. Two weeks before his death in 1919 he described to Nicolas Roerich what America might yet mean to

him personally. "One road open to me," he wrote, "is a journey to America."

> There I deliver lectures against the Bolsheviki, travel through the States, produce my plays, sell my *Satan's Diary* to a publisher, and return a multimillionaire to Russia for a care-free, venerable old age. The trip may turn out a failure (I may be sick, and collapse after the first lecture, or the Americans simply may not care to listen to me), but, under happy conditions, it may prove a "triumphant march": I shall meet people who love me, shall receive impulses for new artistic work. . . . America! But how to get there?

See Leonid Andreyev, *Satan's Diary,* trans. Herman Bernstein (New York: Boni & Liveright, 1920), p. xii, and Alexander Haun, *Leonid Andreyev* (New York: B. W. Heubsch, 1924), pp. 25n, 170-171.

48. Ilya Ehrenburg, *Julio Jurenito,* trans. Anna Bostock and Yvonne Kapp (London: Macgibbon & Kee, 1958), p. 177.

49. Ibid., p. 28. After a ludicrous first visit to a prostitute, one of the characters is greeted by his schoolchum-guide: "Well, what did you think of it? A bit of all right, eh? It's my discovery, I'm a kind of Columbus, you know" (p. 54).

50. I. A. Bunin, *The Gentleman from San Francisco and Other Stories,* trans. D. H. Lawrence, S. S. Koteliansky, and Leonard Woolf (New York: Thomas Seltzer, 1923), p. 57.

51. *Pep: J. L. Wetcheek's American Song Book,* trans. Dorothy Thompson (New York: Viking Press, 1929), pp. viii-ix.

52. Very few of these novels are available in this country. I have relied here on Shalom Weyl, *North America . . . in German Literature, 1918-1945* (unpublished dissertation, Toronto, 1952), pp. 287-330.

53. Valentin Kataev, *Time, Forward!,* trans. Charles Malamuth (New York: Farrar & Rinehart, 1933), p. 126. In 1966 at the age of sixty-nine, Kataev published a thoroughly uncharacteristic story in *Novyj mir,* "Svjatoj kolodec" ("The Sacred Well"). For a provocative if inconclusive discussion of this surrealist fable and

its dream America, see Alayne P. Reilly, *America in Contemporary Soviet Literature* (New York: New York University Press, 1971), pp. 117-171.

54. *Time, Forward!*, p. 128.

55. Ibid., p. 86.

56. Letter of 30 December 1913, trans. by Eudo C. Mason, in *Rilke, Europe, and the English-Speaking World* (Cambridge, Eng.: Cambridge University Press, 1961), p. 161.

57. Trans. Mason, p. 156. What Rilke feared in the machine and in what he called *American* can be seen in these two letters:

> In the present age . . . when everything seems to be volatized and rarified . . . when almost everywhere material catastrophes have taken the place of events permeated with spirit, it is the indefatigable, indifferent *machine* that represents what survives of the visible world; it is what one sees, it and its nasty products and super-products, born, without love, of an invention which takes nothing into account except profit, so much so that it succeeds in ignoring the vital and human meaning of a thing. (Trans. Mason, pp. 164-165.)

This was written in January 1926. In November of 1925 Rilke had written another letter which anticipated much of this while revealing how closely he identified America with "the present age." He laments the

> vanishing of so much that is visible, whose place will not be supplied. Even for our grandparents a "House," a "Well," a familiar tower, their very dress, their cloak, was infinitely more, infinitely more intimate: almost everything a vessel in which they found and stored humanity. Now there come crowding over from America empty, indifferent things, pseudo-things. *Dummy-Life.* . . . A house, in the American understanding, an American apple or vine, has *nothing* in common with the house, the fruit, the grape into which the hope and meditation of our forefathers had entered. . . . The animated experienced things that *share our lives* are coming to an end and cannot be replaced. (Trans. Mason, p. 163.)

"It weighs heavily," Eudo Mason remarks, "that Rilke will not allow American apples to be real apples in his sense. He was a great apple eater, apples had for him a symbolic, quasi-sacramental significance" (p. 242). Mason discusses Rilke's attitude toward the machine at length; Rilke was no sentimental primitive and could even praise the machine, metaphysically, for its mere existence and for its challenge to the poet.

58. Rainer Maria Rilke, *Duino Elegies,* trans. J. B. Leishman and Stephen Spender (New York: W. W. Norton, 1963), pp. 61-63.

59. Klaus Mann, "Dream America," *Accent,* 8 (1948), 173.

60. See Durand Echeverria, *Mirage in the West* (Princeton: Princeton University Press, 1957), p.xiii.

61. See Leon Trotsky, "Novelist and Politician," *The Atlantic Monthly,* 156 (1935), 413-420.

62. Irving Howe, "Céline: The Sod Beneath the Skin," *The New Republic* (July 20, 1963), 20.

63. Duhamel, p. 111.

64. Ibid., pp. 24-25, 27.

65. Cf. C. E. Andrews, "French Authors Take Revenge," *The Bookman,* 73 (March 1931), 19.

66. Louis-Ferdinand Céline, *Journey to the End of the Night,* trans. John H. Marks (New York: New Directions, 1960), pp. 200-201, 352.

67. Ibid., pp. 222, 223, 222-223.

68. Ibid., p. 230.

69. Quoted in "A Man and His Novels," *Times Literary Supplement* (September 15, 1961), 612.

70. *The Moon and the Bonfire,* trans. Louise Sinclair (Harmonsworth, Middlesex: Penguin Books, 1963), pp. 100, 55, 100.

71. Ibid., pp. 56, 53.

72. Cesare Pavese, "Yesterday and Today," *L'Unità* (Turin) (August 3, 1947); reprinted and translated in Heiney, p. 247. Cf. *Cesare Pavese: American Literature,* trans. Edwin Fussell (Berkeley & Los Angeles: University of California Press, 1970), p. 198.

73. Yves Berger, *The Garden,* trans. Robert Baldick (New York: Signet Books, 1963), pp. 17-18.

74. Ibid., pp. 18-19.

75. Ibid., p. 135.

76. David Lodge, "Illusion and Reality," *The Spectator,* vol. 211, p. 433.

77. Jean-Paul Sartre, *Three Plays,* trans. Kitty Black (London: Hamish Hamilton, 1949). Throughout the play, Sartre associates the southern community of his story with the hypocrisy of the whited sepulcher. Although she is a prostitute in flight from trouble in New York, his heroine is yet kind, good, truthful . . . golden-hearted. When she gives herself to Fred, a respected citizen of the town, she does so because she likes him; her essential innocence remains untouched. It is Fred who uses her, who behaves like a beast and can only approach her in the dark. He talks, she says, like a minister, and when he says their bed "stinks of sin," she muses, "I'd never have thought of that." By the play's end she has had to accept the image Fred and the Senator force upon her: she will become Fred's chattel in a house behind the garden, and he will sneak out to visit her at night.

Chapter V

1. George Reavey and Marc Slonim, eds. and trans., *Soviet Literature: An Anthology* (New York: Covici, Friede, 1934), p. 338.

2. *The Brothers Karamazov,* p. 899.

3. *Julio Jurenito,* pp. 74, 85.

4. See Henry Steele Commager, ed., *America in Perspective* (New York: New American Library, 1962), p. 302.

5. Most of the poems discussed in the next few pages appear in Vladimir Mayakovsky, *Polnoe Sobranie Sochinenij,* 7 (Moscow: Goslitizdat, 1958). Unless otherwise indicated, I have relied on translations supplied me by Karen Aharonian and Elizabeth Henderson.

6. Herbert Marshall, "Introduction: Mayakovsky and His Poetry," *Mayakovsky,* trans. Herbert Marshall (New York: Hill and Wang, 1965), pp. 18, 40.

7. In his autobiography Mayakovsky claimed that Gorky "wet my whole waistcoat with tears" when he heard "The Cloud in Trousers" in 1915. Gorky called him a "wonderful lyrical poet."

See *The Bedbug and Selected Poetry,* ed. Patricia Blake (New York: Meridian Books, 1960), p. 305, and Marshall, p. 55. For Mayakovsky's reliance on Gorky in *150,000,000,* see Valentin Kiparsky, *English and American Characters in Russian Fiction* (Berlin: Osteuropa-Institut an der Freien Universitat Berlin, 1964), p. 120.

8. Marshall, pp. 31, 32, 58.

9. Leon Trotsky, *Literature and Revolution* (New York: Russell & Russell, n.d.). pp. 153, 156.

10. Ibid., p. 150.

11. See Zbigniew Folejewski, "Mayakovsky and Futurism," *Comparative Literature Studies,* Special Advance Number (1963), p. 76. Edward J. Brown finds many echoes of Whitman in Mayakovsky's verse but warns against pressing the resemblance too far. See *Mayakovsky: A Poet in the Revolution* (Princeton, N.J.: Princeton University Press, 1973), pp. 89, 115, 171, 177, 182-183.

12. See Marshall, pp. 47-48. Marshall notes that Mayakovsky could have known an earlier translation by Balmont.

13. For a refreshingly breezy, yet authoritative account of Mayakovsky's English, see Hugh McLean, "On Mr. Point Kicč and his Ruptured Russian. . . ," *For Roman Jakobson,* compiled by Morris Halle and others (The Hague: Mouton & Co., 1956), pp. 332-343.

14. The details of Mayakovsky's visit are discussed by McLean, ibid., and by Charles A. Moser, "Mayakovsky's Unsentimental Journeys," *American Slavic and East European Review,* 19 (February 1960), 85-100, and "Mayakovsky and America," *The Russian Review* 25 (July 1966), 242-256. I am indebted in this section to an unpublished translation of Mayakovsky's "My Discovery of America" (1925-26) shown me by Professor Moser.

15. Cf. Ehrenburg's *Julio Jurenito,* pp. 256-257.

16. Cf. Gorky, p. 105.

17. Marshall, p. 141. The lines appear on one of Mayakovsky's posters: for discussion of Marshall's translations, see Guy Daniels, "Project Mayakovsky," *New Republic* (December 4, 1965), 24-28, and Helen Muchnic, "Larger Than Life," *The New York Review of Books* (March 17, 1966), 4.

18. The lines from "100%" appear in Kiparsky, p. 113.

19. Marshall, p. 391.

20. Blake, pp. 173, 177-179, 181.

21. From *My Discovery of America.*

22. From "Christopher Columbus." His spelling reflects Mayakovsky's belief that Columbus was a Spanish Jew; see Moser, "Mayakovsky's Unsentimental Journeys," p. 91.

23. The three poems can be found in *The Poetry of Yevgeny Yevtushenko: 1953 to 1965,* trans. George Reavey (New York: October House, 1965), pp. 121, 125, 117. Yevtushenko describes his proposed American collection in his introduction to *Yevtushenko Poems,* trans. Herbert Marshall (New York: E. P. Dutton, 1966), p. 12. There is a lengthy appreciation of Yevtushenko and his "cryptography" in Alayne P. Reilly, *America in Contemporary Soviet Literature* (New York: New York University Press, 1971), pp. 173-204.

24. Quoted in Reilly, p. 203n4.

25. Herbert Marshall, "The Poet in Russia," *Voznesensky: Selected Poems,* trans. Herbert Marshall (New York: Hill and Wang, 1966), pp. xxix-xxx.

26. See *Yevtushenko Poems,* pp. 11-12, and Anselm Hollo, "An Introduction," *Selected Poems of Andrei Voznesensky,* trans. Anselm Hollo (New York: Grove Press, 1964), pp. 10-11.

27. Hollo, p. 13, and Andrei Voznesensky, *Antiworlds,* ed. Patricia Blake and Max Hayward, trans. William Jay Smith (New York: Basic Books, 1966), p. 106.

28. Marshall, pp. 97-99.

29. *Antiworlds,* pp. 64-65, 69, 72.

30. Anthony Austin, "Talk with Andrei Voznesensky," *New York Times Book Review* (May 14, 1967), p. 5.

31. *Antiworlds,* pp. 74, 66-67, 38.

32. Andrei Voznesensky, "Poem with a Footnote: To Robert Lowell," *The New York Review of Books* (May 18, 1967), p. 21 (trans. Louis Simpson, with Vera Dunham).

33. Harvey W. Hewett-Thayer, *The Modern German Novel* (Boston: Marshall Jones Co., 1924), p. 2.

34. Cf. P. Margot Levi, "K., an Exploration of the Names of Kafka's Central Characters," *Names,* 14 (1966), 1-10.

35. Possible sources for Kafka's America are discussed by Mark Spilka (Franklin and Dickens) and Lienhard Bergel (Whitman)

in *Franz Kafka Today,* ed. Angel Flores and Homer Swander (Madison: University of Wisconsin Press, 1958), pp. 95-127. See especially E. W. Tedlock, Jr., "Kafka's Imitation of David Copperfield," *Comparative Literature,* 7 (Winter 1955), 52-62. For a comparison of *Amerika* with Oscar Handlin's *The Uprooted,* see my "A View from Back Home: Kafka's *Amerika,"* *American Quarterly,* 12 (1961), 33-42. For a similar and less limited approach, see Parker Tyler, "Kafka's 'and Chaplin's 'Amerika,' " *Sewanee Review,* 58 (1950), 299-311.

36. *Amerika,* trans. Edwin Muir (Garden City, N.Y.: Doubleday Anchor Books, 1955), p. 16.

37. Ibid., p. 54.

38. Ibid., p. 64.

39. Ibid., p. 106.

40. Ibid., p. 47.

41. Gustav Janouch, *Conversation with Kafka,* trans. Daroneoy Rees (London: Derek Verschoyle, 1953), p. 85.

42. *Amerika,* pp. 299-300.

43. Sol Gittleman, "Frank Wedekind's Image of America," *German Quarterly,* 39 (1966), 577. There is also the thoroughly contemptible American female. Wedekind describes Wanda Washington of *Oaha* as *durch und durch unecht.* Wedekind fostered the use of mime, dance, and deliberate exaggeration on the stage, and he proved an important influence on the young Brecht. Brecht began his career as a conscious imitator and often visited theater classes conducted by Wedekind's friend and biographer, Arthur Kutscher. Brecht wrote an obituary article when Wedekind died in 1918.

44. After his visit in 1941 as an exile from Hitler and after the commercial failure of *Arturo Ui,* the play he hoped would win him an American audience, Brecht's long artistic dependence upon American correlatives came to a close. He never again employed his grotesque American image. For a note on contemporary sources for Brecht's imagery, see John Willett, *The Theatre of Bertolt Brecht* (London: Methuen & Co., 1959), pp. 66 ff. Willett describes the Americanized Berlin the playwright saw in the 1920s and suggests that the spurious Anglo-Saxon mythology which aped America's Jazz Age might well have reflected the

postwar impact of American economic and technical aid. Whatever the cause, what in Fitzgerald seems arrested adolescence was
duplicated in a far more sophisticated Berlin as an exotic fad:
Berthold Brecht became "Bert" and Georg Grosz "George"; jazz,
"Virginia" cigars, and sport became necessities of life; and
American movies and novels helped people the arts with cowboys
and Indians, Chicago mobsters and girls from the Salvation
Army. It is this America that Brecht drew upon in much of his
early work. (There were related implications in Brecht's two
name changes. Born Bert*hold,* he dropped the suffix "soft,"
"kind." When he later drifted from the mannered Americanism
of the 1920s, he rejected Bert for Bertolt, still avoiding the un-
congenial suffix.) For an earlier version of the present essay, see
Richard Ruland, "The American Plays of Bertolt Brecht,"
American Quarterly, XV (1963); for a recent study, see Helfried
Werner Seliger *Das Amerikabild Bertolt Brechts* (Bonn: Bouvier
Verlag, 1974).

45. *A Little Organum for the Theater,* trans. Beatrice Gottlieb,
Accent, 11 (1951), 16.

46. *In the Swamp: A Boxing Match between Two Men in the Giant City
of Chicago,* trans. Eric Bentley, in *Seven Plays by Bertolt Brecht,* ed.
Eric Bentley (New York: Grove Press, 1961), pp. 22-23.

47. Ibid., p. 46.

48. Ibid., p. 34.

49. Ibid., p. 19.

50. Ibid., p. 25.

51. Ibid., p. 68.

52. Ibid., p. 46.

53. Ibid., p. 61.

54. "Lotte Lenya Remembers Mahagonny," in the booklet
which accompanies the Columbia recording of the opera. The
booklet also contains Guy Stern's translation, and I have used it
in the discussion which follows. The recorded version occasionally
differs from that collected in *Stücke III.*

55. *A Man's a Man,* trans. Eric Bentley, *Seven Plays,* p. 82.

56. I am grateful to Professor Frank Jones for his kind advice
and for his translation of Brecht's poem, "Vanished Glory of New
York, the Giant City." It appeared in *Diogenes* (Madison, Wis.), 1
(October-November 1940), 21-26.

57. *Kriegsfibel,* p. 38 (trans. Willett).

58. *Seven Plays,* p. xvi.

59. Quoted in Martin Esslin, *Brecht: The Man and His Work* (Garden City, N.Y.: Doubleday Anchor Books, 1961), p. 159.

60. *Saint Joan of the Stockyards,* trans. Frank Jones, *Seven Plays,* p. 151. There are remarkable parallels in both this play and *Seven Sins* to Act 4 of Ibsen's *Peer Gynt* (1867). Ibsen described this anomolous fourth act as an afterthought.

61. Ibid., p. 153.

62. Ibid., p. 155.

63. Ibid., p. 170.

64. Ibid., p. 178.

65. Ibid., p. 217. Cf. the strike scene in Zola's *Germinal* (1885).

66. Ibid., pp. 224-225.

67. Ibid., pp. 235, 251.

68. Ibid., pp. 254-255.

69. I have used the unsigned translation which accompanies the Capitol recording of *The Seven Deadly Sins of the Petty Bourgeois (Anna Anna)* in preference to the freer rendering by W. H. Auden.

70. *The Resistible Rise of Arturo Ui,* trans. H. R. Hays; unpublished, but available on microfilm at Columbia University library. Brecht's plays were not the first to investigate German politics from the vantage point of America. Shalom Weyl discusses *Thomas Paine* (1927) by the right-wing Hanns Johst, who "changes the whole character of the hero to fit him into the current ideology. Much is omitted, shortened, and changed by 'poetic freedom', so that the real man and the American background are so reduced as to leave nothing but the colour of a very modern type of German emotional nationalist. The whole," Weyl complains, is "imbued with Führer-mentality" (p. 322). Yet another expressionist playwright to use America was Georg Kaiser; Kaiser's values were much closer to Brecht's than were Johst's. In *Mississippi* (1930), Kaiser's tight drama of personal regeneration is worked out in a struggle between the poor whites of the delta and the selfish capitalists of New Orleans.

And Kaiser's *Napoleon in New Orleans* (1944) is a rollicking attack on fascism which echoes the method, the wit, and the point of Brecht's *Arturo Ui* (1941). There is a touch of Pirandello, too, in the dramaturgical setting Kaiser provides for this examination of appearance and reality. Baron Dergan's passion for Napoleon invites the stratagem adopted by the group of swindlers who dupe him. But although he and his daughter are robbed of their physical well-being, they retain our sympathy through a triumphant integrity—particularly once they reject their foolishness and the fascistic destruction of America it entails. The actor who manipulates their credulity is not simply a sham in his own person; the Napoleon he plays (and, by extension, any dictator of whatever time or place) is revealed as equally unreal, a self-willed creation of those who cry to be imposed upon. Of all the characters in the play, only the poseur understands the situation fully. When a confederate compliments him on the skill with which he portrays Napoleon, the actor responds with a scathing portrait of the totalitarian leader:

If you take what I am doing here for art, then you don't have the slightest notion of art. That is a role [i.e., playing dictator] which the most wretched comedian can bring off. Precisely because it is so wretched. It is composed of the most inferior elements. Cruelty, vulgarity, breach of promise, baseness in every form, envy, hate, treason, open and secret murder—I do not need to enumerate further. It is those tendencies which are mixed in human nature but have been suppressed through evolution until they finally lie completely dormant. The emperor awakens them again. . . . Are you very astonished now, that I play the role so perfectly? I am a rogue.

Cf. William Eickhorst, "The Treatment of the South in Modern German Literature," *Arizona Quarterly*, 15 (1959), 221-222. See also B. J. Kenworthy, *Georg Kaiser* (Oxford: Basil Blackwell, 1957), pp. 138-140.

71. Emilio Cecchi, *America Amara* (Florence: Sansoni, 1946), p. 140; trans. Donald Heiney, *America in Modern Italian Literature* (New Brunswick, N.J.: Rutgers University Press, 1964), p. 39.

72. Mario Soldati, *America Primo Amora* (Milan: Garganti, 1956), p. 65; trans. Heiney, p. 32.

73. *The Capri Letters,* trans Archibald Colquhoun (New York: Alfred A. Knopf, 1956), p. 248.

74. Ibid., p. 251.

75. Ibid., pp. 3-4.

76. Ibid., p. 304.

77. Ibid., p. 83.

78. Ibid., p. 36.

79. Ibid., pp. 32-33.

80. Ibid., p. 33.

81. Ibid., p. 35.

82. Ibid., p. 54.

83. Ibid., p. 39.

84. Ibid., p. 132.

85. Ibid., p. 174.

86. Ibid., p. 280.

87. Ibid., pp. 272-273.

88. Ibid., p. 23.

89. Ibid., p. 297.

90. Ibid., p. 304.

91. Ibid., p. 298.

92. Ibid., p. 248

93. Ibid., p. 311.

94. Simon Jeune, *De F. T. Graindorge à A.O. Barnabooth: Les Types Américains dans le Roman et le Théâtre Français (1861-1917),* (Paris: Didier, 1963), p. 458.

95. See, for example, Julian Green, *Diary: 1928-1957,* trans. Anne Green (New York: Harcourt, Brace & World, 1964), p. 132.

96. Julian Green, *Personal Record: 1928-1939,* trans. Jocelyn Godefroi (New York: Harper & Bros., 1939), p. 206.

97. *Diary,* pp. 48-49.

98. Ibid., pp. 50-51.

99. *Personal Record,* pp. 155-56. Green thought Hawthorne "one of the greatest writers of his time." "What endears him to me particularly is the value he gives to silence and all the invisible." See *Diary,* pp. 116-117.

100. *Personal Record,* pp. 194-196.

101. Ibid., p. 212. Green's reason for leaving *The Distant Countries* unfinished is relevant to the subject of the present study.

He had chosen as setting, he says, "the most romantic of all the forest scenery of the New World." But he did not feel at ease with the concrete details of time, boredom, vain striving, and restlessness he needed. His work was becoming less a genuinely creative fiction and more "an 'historical novel novel,' " which seemed to paralyze his powers of invention. "I am afraid," he remarks in rejecting the elementary effects of local color, "I am afraid of subsiding into some dreadful historical rechauffe." (ibid., pp. 185, 193). By 1953 he was more willing to exploit the historical south; see *Sud: pièce en trois actes* (Paris: Plon, 1953).

102. A detail perhaps suggested by a similar reticence in Hawthorne; see *Diary,* p. 117.

103. Ibid., pp. 82, 221.

104. Ibid., p. 302.

105. Julian Green, *Each in His Darkness,* trans. Anne Green (New York: Pantheon Books, 1961), p. 9.

106. Ibid., pp. 11, 26.

107. Ibid., p. 224.

108. Ibid., pp. 98, 163.

109. Ibid., pp. 62-63.

110. Ibid., p. 16.

111. Ibid., p. 10.

112. Paul Claudel, "A Poem by St.-John Perse," in St.-John Perse, *Winds,* trans. Hugh Chisholm (New York: Pantheon Books, 1953), pp. 234, 224.

113. Ibid., p. 234.

114. Archibald MacLeish, "The Personality of St.-John Perse," in St.-John Perse, *Exile and Other Poems,* trans. Denis Devlin (New York: Pantheon Books, 1949), p. 145.

115. Julian Green, *Diary: 1928-1957,* trans. Anne Green (New York: Harcourt, Brace & World, 1964), p. 196.

116. *Exile and Other Poems,* p. 138.

117. *Winds,* p. 124.

118. Ibid., p. 152.

119. Ibid., p. 181.

120. Ibid., pp. 184-185.

121. Julian Green, *Personal Record: 1928-1939,* trans. Jocelyn Godefroi (New York: Harper & Bros., 1939), p. 285.

122. *Winds,* p. 163.

123. Giame Pintor, "Americana," *Aretusa,* 2 (1945); reprinted and trans. by Heiney, p. 238.

Epilogue

1. Cf. Sigmund Skard, *The American Myth and the European Mind* (Philadelphia: University of Pennsylvania Press, 1961), p. 7.

2. Durand Echeverria, "The Use of the John Carter Brown Library in Fields Other than History," *The John Carter Brown Library Conference* (Providence, R.I., 1961), p. 47.

3. Walter Kaufmann, *Critique of Religion and Philosophy* (New York: Harper & Brothers, 1958), pp. 66-67. Cf. Howard Nemerov: "The poet is in the ancient word for him a *maker,* and he doesn't foretell the future, he makes it, he brings it to pass, he sings it up. It becomes his dream." "Poetry, Prophecy, Prediction," *Reflexions on Poetry & Poetics* (New Brunswick, N.J.: Rutgers University Press, 1972), p. 218.

4. Nemerov, p. 221.

INDEX